THE WILLIAM WORDSWORTH WAY

The William Wordsworth Way

HOWARD BECK

MAINSTREAM
PUBLISHING

EDINBURGH AND LONDON

The wisest, happiest, of our kind are they
That ever walk content with Nature's way

William Wordsworth

First published in 1998 by
MAINSTREAM PUBLISHING COMPANY (EDINBURGH) LTD
7 Albany Street
Edinburgh EH1 3UG

ISBN 1 85158 978 3

A catalogue record for this book is available from the
British Library

Photographs by Howard Beck
Typeset in Sabon and Arial
Printed and bound in Great Britain by The Cromwell Press Ltd

CONTENTS

Acknowledgements

I am indebted to my long-standing friend Peter Rose for kindly transporting me and my rucksack to the starting point, and for being supportive when needed. I am also grateful to Andy Roberts and all the people, including other walkers, who offered help or encouragement along the way. I wish to thank Denis Round and Sheila Mitton for their hospitality before the start of the walk, and the staff of the Seatoller youth hostel for taking in one bedraggled backpacker on a wild, wet night.

Introduction

The Lakes, as they are now affectionately known, hold a special place in the history of the north, from the earliest Stone Age up to the present, having been important to man as a provider of food and shelter, and a source of raw materials and inspiration. As a place of infinite beauty, too, the Lakes have inspired writers, artists and poets; Lear, Westall, Turner, Constable, Gainsborough, Southey and Wordsworth are some of the more famous names whose work evokes the very essence of all that is typical of the northern British countryside.

William Wordsworth was born at Cockermouth on 7 April 1770, at a time when visitors to the district were relatively scarce. The audacious few who travelled did so out of necessity, and it was not until the middle of the 18th century that the countryside was romanticised, and that the forerunners of the present-day tourists, inspired by such endeavours, came to view the landscape for what it was.

In this respect it is perhaps ironic that while in later life William foresaw the damage that might result from an increase in visitor numbers, he himself was eventually to become one of the area's main attractions. By the beginning of the 19th century the tentative trickle of 'Lakers' had swelled to become a veritable flood, but even then no one could have foretold of the explosion of interest in walking that the area would eventually witness.

To the Wordsworth household, walking was both an accepted necessity and a favoured form of recreation, William himself thinking nothing of covering maybe 30 miles in a single day during the course of visiting friends and relations. Arguably he could be regarded as a genuine forerunner of today's ramblers and, indeed, he was one of the very first to tread on many a Lakeland summit, including the highest, Scafell Pike. It is estimated that he covered over 180,000 miles in his lifetime.

I have always nurtured an interest in walking and a deep

affection for the Lake District scenery in particular, a love affair that has not waned in over 30 years, a period during which I believed I had grown to know the Lakes as well as most. However, my 'discovery' of Wordsworth was akin to acquiring a new pair of eyes with which to view the countryside that makes up this premier National Park. I found after some time that it was impossible, perhaps even undesirable, to view the scenery from outside the context of his verse, this in turn leading to the realisation that the two were quite inseparable.

Background to the Walk

Being a walker who likes to cover many miles in a single journey, I decided that the best way to enjoy the Lake District, and to experience the unique relationship between the scenery and the verse, was to devise a long-distance route that benefited from both. After scrutinising maps and using my knowledge of the region, at last I decided upon a route that would work, a circular walk visiting over 80 sites associated with William Wordsworth, and traversing some of the most stunning landscapes in Britain.

As a starting point for this literary trail, Cockermouth was the obvious choice since this was the poet's birthplace. Deciding upon a suitable itinerary was more difficult. The seemingly simple quest of visiting as many Wordsworthian locations as possible had to be tempered by the practicalities of keeping the route down to a length that would be manageable within a journey of two weeks' duration. I could have included St Bees Head, Furness Abbey, Cartmel Priory and the Duddon estuary, but these would have added considerably to the overall length of the walk.

In the end I opted, somewhat reluctantly, to confine the walk, as much as was practical, to the countryside within the bounds of the Lake District National Park. Even so, it departs at two points, for instance in visiting Penrith centre and, at the start and finishing point, Cockermouth town itself.

The walk passes through almost every major valley and utilises existing rights of way (for instance, quiet country lanes, bridleways, footpaths, farm tracks, old coaching roads, evocative Roman military highways and sinister corpse roads). Some sections are coincident with parts of other long-distance walks, for example the Cumbria Way, Allerdale Ramble, the Coast to Coast Walk and the Lakeland 3000s walk. The route includes tarns, high mountain summits and ridges, rock-girt passes, waterfalls, exposed moors, riversides and lake shores, forests, villages and towns.

Because the William Wordsworth Way is a circular walk, it

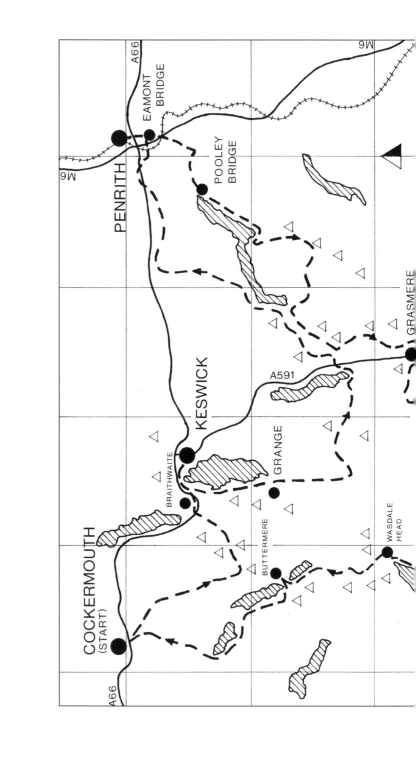

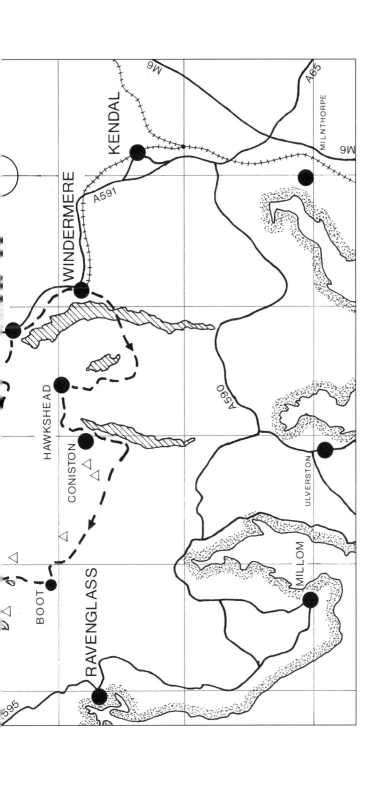

may of course be joined and left at any convenient point. The official starting point, however, is the gate outside Wordsworth House in Cockermouth. Each day's stage has been planned so it ends where accommodation is readily available, for instance campsites, bothies and bunkbarns, youth hostels, B&Bs or hotels. Route variations, where they are thought desirable, are described and notes are provided on the availability of essential supplies.

Without doubt the finest way of undertaking this walk is to take it gently – by this I mean unburdened by the huge loads that seem synonymous with backpacking. There is no shortage of accommodation. By this means walkers shouldering a simple daysack will become immersed in their natural surroundings and enjoy the very essence of the Lakes with which Wordsworth himself would have been familiar.

But – and this is a big but – don't be misled, for overall this walk is a tough undertaking and one that should not be embarked upon lightly. The route is primarily a backpacker's trail covering approximately 180 miles (288 kilometres), and with a total height gain in the order of 26,000 feet (7,924 metres). These figures will fluctuate according to the route variations, and if any of the extra options are chosen. The walk crosses high ground at several places, with the loftiest point attained being on the summit of Helvellyn at 3,116 feet (950 metres).

The walk has been devised so that each stage can be covered in a day; some are short to allow ample time to visit a number of places connected with the poet. Strong walkers could of course double up on certain stages and complete the route in perhaps ten days. Escape routes, where they exist, enable the walker to return to the day's starting point by utilising available public transport. For those who have energy in reserve, diversionary options provide the added opportunity of climbing further Lakeland peaks. The reader is strongly urged both to observe the Countryside Code and to obtain the maximum enjoyment from this walk by referring to the Author's Notes that follow.

Please note that any reference to fees, telephone numbers, time schedules or other information relative to carriers, accommodation, campsites and other attractions was correct at the time of writing. Because this information is liable to change without notice, neither the author nor the publisher can accept any responsibility for inconvenience or loss incurred. For this reason the reader is urged to check in advance to verify such details.

Author's Notes

TRAVELLING TO THE LAKE DISTRICT

There are regular bus services into the Lakes from most large cities and train services to Windermere and Penrith. There are several trains daily to Penrith, via Carlisle from Glasgow and Edinburgh, and from London's Euston Station with connections to Windermere.

From Manchester trains running every two hours from Piccadilly serve Windermere and Penrith, and there are several services daily to Penrith (with connections for Windermere) from Birmingham. Bus service 685 or trains from Newcastle connect at Carlisle with bus service 555 for Keswick and Windermere. Travellers from Leeds can take advantage of a rail service changing at Preston or Lancaster, alternatively via the Settle Carlisle line with a connection at Kirkby Stephen for bus service 888 to Penrith and Keswick.

Several other bus routes serve Lake District centres. Service X88 links Durham with Alston, with onward connections to Penrith and Keswick (Saturday and Wednesday during school summer holidays). Coach service X8 from Leeds (Central Bus Station) calls at Windermere, Ambleside, Grasmere and Keswick on Monday, Thursday and Friday.

A National Coach service is run from London's Victoria Coach Station at 10.30 daily reaching Windermere and Keswick by early evening. Bus connections: at Penrith, service X5 for Keswick and Cockermouth; at Windermere Rail Station, service 555 for Keswick, 599 for Bowness, and 555, 599 for Ambleside and Grasmere. The X9 service route connects York with Keswick via Harrogate, Skipton, Settle, Ingleton, Kirkby Lonsdale, Kendal, Staveley, Windermere, Ambleside and Grasmere.

Before you start the William Wordsworth Way, the relevant operator should be contacted for up-to-date information relating to rail and road services and forward connections into the region. For bus information telephone (01946) 63222; for railway service details, the number is (01539) 720397. For general information on the Internet about transport to and within the Lake District, call http://www.wwwebguides.com/pubtrans/cumbria/info.html

PUBLIC TRANSPORT WITHIN THE LAKES

Reaching the Lake District is relatively easy using public transport. This means that cars do not have to be left unattended for two weeks. Scheduled bus services within the Lakes are quite comprehensive, in summer at least, and are operated by Stagecoach Cumberland, who should be contacted for up-to-date timetables relative to the services shown below.

Service No.555 (Lakeslink) connecting Windermere, Ambleside, Rydal, Grasmere, Wythburn Church and Keswick.

Service No.505/506 (Coniston Rambler) links Windermere, Bowness pier, Ambleside, Skelwith Bridge, Hawkshead and Coniston.

Service No.517 (Kirkstone Rambler) linking Bowness pier, Windermere rail station, Brotherswater, Patterdale Hotel and Glenridding.

Service No.515 links Ambleside, Hawkshead, Grizedale Forest, Newby Bridge, Ulverston and Grange-over-Sands.

Service No.516 links Ambleside to Dungeon Ghyll (Langdale) via Skelwith Bridge, Elterwater and Chapel Stile. Also linking with Kendal and Windermere (Sundays).

Service Nos. X5, 34, 35 links Penrith with Whitehaven via Threlkeld, Keswick, Braithwaite, Bassenthwaite, Workington and Cockermouth.

Service Nos. 77, 77A links Keswick with Buttermere via Grange Bridge, Seatoller, Honister YHA, Lorton and Whinlatter.

Service No.79 links Keswick to Seatoller via Grange Bridge and Rosthwaite.

Service No. 37 links Patterdale with Workington via Glenridding, Threlkeld, Keswick and Cockermouth.

Service No.108 links Penrith with Patterdale serving Yanwath Cottages, Pooley Bridge, Gowbarrow Cottages, Park Brow Foot and Glenridding.

The YHA in the Lake District provides a summer-season shuttle bus carrying people, or their packs, between specific YHA hostels and Windermere rail station. For transport of pack only, a charge of £2 is levied; tickets are available from any hostel taking part in the scheme, i.e. Windermere (High Cross), Hawkshead (Esthwaite Lodge), Coniston (Holly How), Elterwater (Langdale), Grasmere (Thorney How), Ambleside (Waterhead) and Patterdale (Goldrill House).

In addition, the Lakeland Pick-and-Drop service (Tel: 016973 44275/42768) will deliver or collect walkers or their gear anywhere, at any time, by 4x4 vehicle. It is advisable to book well in advance if a walk schedule is known. The Bowness ferry is open all year round (subject to weather) and is an integral link in this circular walk. It usually begins operations at 7 a.m. and runs until around 10 p.m. If closed due to bad weather (a rarity), the alternative is a lengthy journey by road carrier.

On summer Sundays the National Trust operates a free passenger shuttle between Keswick and Watendlath, and from Hawkshead to Tarn Hows. For enquiries Tel: (015394) 35599.

The Ravenglass and Eskdale narrow-gauge railway (Tel: 01229 717171) can be used for the interesting Miterdale variation of the Eskdale to Wasdale stage of the walk. A number of taxi operators serve the Lake District but are too numerous to list here. Walkers should contact Tourist Information Offices for the phone numbers if required.

ACCOMMODATION AND CAMPING
Only in a couple of instances are there no readily accessible official campsites. The position in the Lakes is that there is no legal right to camp, although a *de facto* tradition exists that above the 1,000 feet contour or above intake land camping is okay. Intake is the enclosed, improved land along the valley floor and lower fell slopes. Although frowned upon by some, wild camping is a possibility if discretion is exercised.

Although the route is in essence a backpackers' walk, each stage of it is designed so as to end at or within convenient reach not only of official campsites, but also of other suitable accommodation, such as bunkbarns and hostels. It is possible to travel comfortably light if taking advantage of youth hostels, B&Bs or hotels, or if the Pick-and-Drop service is used. Unless camping, walkers would be well advised to book ahead in order to guarantee a bed. Most youth hostels offer both a meals service and self-catering facilities.

TIME OF YEAR

Autumn is the best period to witness the kaleidoscope of colours on the woodland stages, yet late March is the month to enjoy Wordsworth's carpets of wild daffodils (*Narcissus pseudonarcissus*) in Rydal, and at Gowbarrow beside Ullswater. Unfortunately, these months do not enjoy as much daylight as high summer does, and so consequently some of the lengthier stages would demand a crack-of-doom start and a fast pace to avoid finishing after dusk. Moreover, many campsites do not open until Easter. By May the daffodils are past their best, but the woods are suffused by the ethereal blue haze of the wild hyacinth or bluebell.

Again, because of the short days, attempting the walk in winter is not recommended; however, when seen beneath a mantle of snow the mountain scenery takes on an entirely different appearance. At this time of year those stages crossing high ground will necessitate the carrying of at least an ice axe and possibly crampons, thus further increasing the weight burden. In addition, public transport options will be severely limited.

Without doubt the optimum time of year to tackle the Way is between May and August, bearing in mind that without a suitable deterrent midges in summer can make camping uncomfortable, and that in high season advance bookings will be necessary in order to secure a bed in youth hostels, hotels and guest-houses.

WEATHER

Changing weather patterns over the past two decades have resulted in milder winters and wetter summers. Because the Lakeland mountains are the first high ground encountered by the moisture-laden westerlies blowing in off the Atlantic, rain here is a frequent occurrence. On a walk lasting two weeks anyone not encountering rain will be very lucky.

As this is a mountainous region, the weather can change faster than some walkers realise. In summer, carry a high-factor sunscreen to protect the skin from harmful UV rays and don't forget the midge repellent. Always be prepared for the worst, even in summer, and do not underestimate the awesome power of a thunderstorm. Up-to-date weather information can be accessed by phoning the Lake District National Park 24-hour Weatherline Service on (017687) 75757.

MOUNTAIN SAFETY

Never remain on high ground if a storm threatens: leave summits and ridges as quickly as is safely possible and never shelter beneath a tree, near a cave or mine entrance, in gullies, ravines or near stream channels. All metal objects, including jewellery, should be discarded. The safest place to shelter is generally taken to be in the lee of a large boulder, within a radius equivalent to its height. Don't stand upright, but crouch on all fours with feet, knees and forearms on the ground, insulated from the earth by a rucksack. By this means, if you are unfortunate enough to be struck by lightning, the current should pass relatively harmlessly through the limbs rather than the vital organs such as the heart.

An exposure sack or bivvy bag, spare food, torch, whistle and waterproof/windproof clothing should be carried as standard kit on all walks into remote, high or difficult terrain. It goes without saying, too, that those venturing into such country must observe a mountain code of safety, and in addition should at the very least have a basic working knowledge of first-aid procedures, and also know and observe the Countryside Code.

Many common causes of difficulty are the result of walkers overestimating their own ability, underestimating the time required to complete a walk or section of a walk, having inadequate clothing, boots or nourishment, a lack of foresight and the inability to read a map and compass. Any one or a combination of these factors can produce an exhausted walker who may subsequently become disorientated or overtaken by the dark.

Always take special care to guard against stonefalls. After prolonged rain, many streams can become impossible or dangerous to ford. If there is no bridge, seek a place to cross where the flow is less violent, undo waist straps and sling packs on one shoulder so these can be jettisoned in an emergency. Cross between boulders or shingle banks if possible and use a stick or walking pole to maintain balance, taking a diagonal line into the current. If walking in a group, link arms for additional security.

At present, mountain rescue in Great Britain is provided free of charge by teams of volunteers who are themselves walkers, climbers or mountaineers. If an emergency arises, the mountain rescue service may be alerted by phoning 999 and asking the police for mountain rescue.

Everyone should be familiar with the international distress signals. These are a code of signals first devised in 1894 as a means by which walkers or mountaineers in distress could attract attention. Six blasts of a whistle or flashes of a torch should be repeated after intervals of one minute. If a whistle is not available, an injured or crag-bound walker could summon help by waving a brightly coloured anorak six times. The universal response is three blasts of a whistle or torch flashes at one-minute intervals.

The recognised signals for communicating with a helicopter winchman are as follows: Both hands held outstretched above the head to form a V indicates LAND HERE or HELP NEEDED, and YES (to winchman's questions). One arm only raised means DO NOT LAND HERE, HELP IS NOT NEEDED or NO (to winchman's questions).

CLOTHING AND EQUIPMENT

It is essential to keep the backpack load as light as possible while still being prepared for all eventualities. A lightweight tent is the natural choice for most backpackers, though of course bivvy bags offer an even lighter (but less comfortable) alternative. Basic essentials are a small stove and something to cook with, a sleeping mat, wet-weather clothing, a warm hat and gloves depending on the time of year, at least one spare pair of socks, a water bottle, water sterilisation tablets (optional) and a small first-aid kit. For those with more funds to spare, ample accommodation in youth hostels, guest-houses and hotels will obviate the need for camping gear, thus dramatically cutting the pack weight.

FLORA AND FAUNA

The Lake District enjoys a rich natural heritage providing habitats for many indigenous species, such as red squirrel, fox, badger, roe and red deer. The grey squirrel and feral mink are two much despised introductions. Birds of the high ground are represented by buzzard, peregrine falcon, merlin, raven, ring ouzel and wheatear, while the eastern parts are home to England's sole pair of golden eagles.

Elsewhere, walkers are likely to encounter goldcrest, wren, golden plover, sparrow-hawk, skylark, kestrel, jay, green and great spotted woodpecker, swallow, all three species of wagtail, nuthatch, tree-creeper and several species of finch and tit. The many lakes, rivers and tarns attract numerous species of water fowl; grey lag goose, Canada goose, gooseander, heron, dipper, mallard, tufted duck, goldeneye, whooper swan, coot and moorhen are representative.

Of all the wild blooms it is with thanks to Wordsworth that the district is known best for its daffodils. The diversity of landscape supports a great variety of flowers, however, some rare species survive in a few isolated localities, notably the red alpine catchfly (*Lychnis viscaria*) found on Hobcarton Crag, the eastern flank of Hopegill Head.

Amongst the many blooms walkers can expect to find (depending upon time of year) are primrose (*Primula vulgaris*), bluebell (*Endymion non-scriptus*), wood sorrel (*Oxalis acetosella*), foxgloves (*Digitalis purporea*), yellow flag (*Iris pseudacorus*), dog violet (*Viola riviniana*), ivy-leafed toadflax (*Cymbalaria muralis*), anemones (*Anemone nemorosa*), marsh marigold (*Caltha palustris*), starry saxifrage (*Saxifraga stellaris*) and bugle (*Ajuga repans*).

PHOTOGRAPHY

The Lake District is a superbly picturesque region presenting limitless opportunities for landscape study. Though most walkers would probably shun the carrying of a multi-lens system, if using a 35mm outfit a wide-angle lens with a field of view not less than 35mm is a boon. With space at a premium, however, and forever conscious of pack weight, a compromise would be to use the 35mm camera in conjunction with a macro-zoom; alternatively, there are many excellent compact cameras on the market.

The use of a skylight or ultra-violet filter will improve colour rendition in the mountains, while a polarising filter can be used to control reflections in lake shots. For black-and-white film, the use of an orange filter will improve the appearance of clouds, and give greater clarity over distance. A green filter helps differentiate individual nuances of foliage in woodland scenes.

In all probability more film will be used than is anticipated but it is not necessary to carry huge stocks since the route takes in several centres where films can be bought. Process-paid films, once exposed, can be posted at the earliest opportunity to reduce weight and avoid the possibility of damaging them through exposure to damp or heat.

Walkers should note that it is not usually possible, without prior arrangement, to take photographs within museums, National Trust buildings and those properties associated with Wordsworth.

Using the Guide

Each stage of the walk is provided with a clearly drawn map and associated altitude profile to help the walker determine the nature and relative difficulty of each day. The descriptions open with a summary of the terrain to be crossed, highlighting any difficulties or attractions, noting which maps will be required, the distance and altitude gained and an estimate of how long the stage will take to complete.

The times shown for each stage should be taken as a guide only, for the obvious reason that everyone walks at a different pace according to fitness, experience, the weather, the nature of the terrain and the load being shouldered. Throughout the route, notes are provided to help the walker benefit from the Wordsworthian associations of the landscape. To make for clarity in using the main body text, any detailed notes not directly related to the route description are preceded by the symbol >>. This indicates that the reader will find the continuing route directions where the next instance of this symbol is found.

MAPS AND ROUTE-FINDING

The reader is referred to the 1:25000 Outdoor Leisure Series maps produced by the Ordnance Survey. The Lake District is covered on four sheets, all of which it will be necessary to use. Though these maps are excellent in detail, they are of a size that makes them unmanageable in the slightest breeze. A number of companies are now producing these maps in a laminated, waterproof form that is well worth the extra cost since it is simplicity itself to write off a map in a single day of bad weather.

Most of the route is well waymarked with the standard footpath and bridleway signs, as well as with yellow and blue direction arrows respectively. No difficulties should be experienced if the description in this guide is followed in conjunction with the relevant Ordnance Survey maps. Some stages do, however, cross exposed mountain country and open fellsides. For this reason it is imperative that the walker is conversant in the use of map and compass, and has the confidence to use them in poor visibility. The stage between the Duddon Valley and Eskdale crosses woods that have been recently logged and where the route may as a result be difficult to follow.

The advent of satellite technology has provided the outdoor enthusiast with the GPS receiver, an electronic navigation aid specifying the user's position to within a few yards. Although innovative, the extra weight of the GPS prohibits its use for most backpacking circumstances, and in any event there is no substitute for good navigational know-how the old-fashioned way. More and more outdoors enthusiasts seem to be packing mobile phones, though the mountain rescue service should only be summoned if self-rescue is not a viable option.

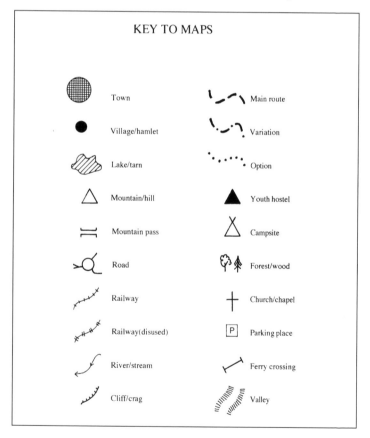

ROUTE SUMMARY

DAY	STAGE	DISTANCE (Miles)	ALTITUDE GAIN (Feet)	DURATION (Hours)
1	Cockermouth–Keswick	16.75	1,879	5–6
2	Keswick–Longthwaite	9	82	3–6
3	Longthwaite–Glenridding	13	4,117	6–7
4	Glenridding–Eamont Br	18.5	2,559	8
5	Eamont Br–Pooley Br	9.5	236	3
6	Pooley Br–Patterdale	18	2,795	6–7
7	Patterdale–Grasmere	14.5	3,100	6
8	Grasmere–Elterwater	12.75	2,601	4–5
9	Elterwater–High Cross	9.75	1,115	3
10	High Cross–Coniston	19	1,581	7–8
11	Coniston–Eskdale	15.75	2,723	5–7
12	Eskdale–Wasdale Head	5.5	820	2
13	Wasdale Head–Buttermere	8	2,165	3–4
14	Buttermere–Cockermouth	13	797	6

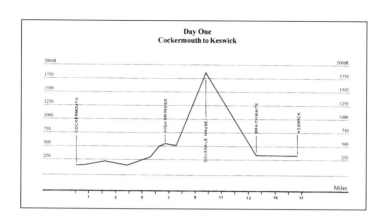

Day One
Cockermouth to Keswick

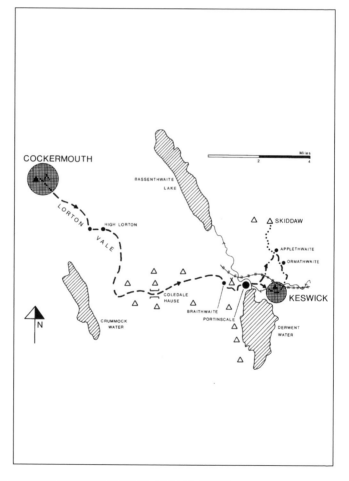

THE WILLIAM WORDSWORTH WAY

DAY 1
Cockermouth to Keswick

SUMMARY
Distance: 13.75 miles (to Braithwaite campsite). Add a
   further 3 miles to Keswick YHA.
Total Ascent: 1,879 feet (573 metres).
Expected Duration: 5–6 hours.
Map: 1:25000 Outdoor Leisure Series sheet No.4.
Terrain and Difficulty: Easy and pleasant walking through
   Lorton Vale forms the precursor to a steady ascent over
   Coledale Hause, a pass leading into Coledale, through
   which the last stage threads its way.
Highlights: Excellent mountain views and quiet villages.
Option: Cockermouth town trail (allow 1 hour, plus extra
   time if entering Wordsworth House).

This, the first stage of the walk, begins outside the imposing
Georgian house that once was the residence of the Wordsworths. Since Cockermouth has many associations with this
famous family, the walker is urged not to be impetuous, but
instead to take sufficient time to explore the short town
trail described below before dashing off to begin this fine
walk.

Those planning to stay overnight in Cockermouth in
readiness for an early start the following morning will find an
ample choice of hotel and B&B accommodation there.
Moreover, the youth hostel and campsite are easily reached
from the centre, both being located on the south side of town
within convenient walking distance of Wordsworth House, on
Main Street. Last-minute supplies will be found in a varied
selection of shops. >>

Cockermouth town occupies the angle formed by the confluence of two rivers, the Cocker and the larger Derwent. It
was granted its first market charter as long ago as 1221, but
has not lost any of its colourful Cumberland charm over the
intervening centuries, imparting still the impression of a well-

to-do place, the bright and cheery market town that it was during Wordsworth's childhood.

William was born in 1770 to John Wordsworth, legal adviser and land agent to Sir James Lowther, head of one of the most influential families in the north of England at that time. Wordsworth House, the poet's birthplace, remains one of the most imposing buildings along Main Street, and is owned today by the National Trust who have opened it to the public. Across the road from the house will be seen a bust of the poet paid for and erected by the town's Rotary Round Table and Lions Club.

Down the centuries Cockermouth has occupied a strategic position, the presence of a castle reflecting local insecurities, guarding as it does the town's north-eastern approach. It provided the inspiration for verse that was redolent of childhood days, when both William and his sister, Dorothy, played in the ruins and were frightened by the 'soul-appalling darkness' discovered in the dungeons. *Address from the Spirit of Cockermouth Castle* is a poem that graphically illustrates the young Wordsworths' experience.

The original structure, dating from 1134, is credited to Waltheof, son of Gospatric, one-time Earl of Dunbar. The existing structure is said to be a 13th-century reconstruction, using stones apparently 'borrowed' from the Roman fort at nearby Derventio (Papcastle).

Like so many fortifications, it has had a troubled past. Harassed by marauding Scots under Robert the Bruce, it was later held alternatively by the Houses of Lancaster and York during the Wars of the Roses, and was, in addition, used by Parliamentary troops during the Civil War. Since then, the castle has been left at the mercy of the elements, although amazingly parts of it still remain habitable today and are owned by the Dowager Lady Egremont.

Cockermouth, of course, had two famous sons. One, Fletcher Christian (*c*.1764–*c*.1794), achieved rather more infamy in later years, leading the mutiny on the *Bounty*, an event that for some South Sea islands changed the course of history. But it is William Wordsworth, the Lakes poet, for which the town and the Lake District are more widely known, and after whom this literary trail has been named.

From Wordsworth House walk 50 yards east up Main Street and turn left into the narrow confines of Bridge Street, here giving access, via a footbridge, to a footpath beside the River Derwent. The northern aspect of the castle can be glimpsed from the riverbank but is almost crowded out by the adjacent brewery, the best views being obtained upstream by the first

This bust of the poet stands on the corner opposite Wordsworth House in Cockermouth, starting point for the William Wordsworth Way

bend. Even further upriver are the fields of yellow ragwort (*Senecio jaconaea*) through which the boy William romped and chased butterflies with his sister, and to which the poem *To a Butterfly*, composed in 1802, refers.

Return to the footbridge and continue downstream through the Memorial Gardens to the road bridge. From here to the north-east can be seen Watch Hill, a sight referred to in the poet's *The Prelude*, and one which fascinated young William so, of a 'road' climbing over its brow like an invitation into the unknown.

Continuing from the road bridge, walk along to and turn left into Main Street once again, proceeding past the gate of Wordsworth House. Walk along the broad avenue – it will be bustling on a Saturday – passing Bridge Street and the Earl of Mayo Monument, to where Market Place veers off right. This leads into the oldest quarters of the town. On the left by this junction the Cumberland Toy and Model Museum can be reached down a narrow ginnel.

To reach All Saints Church where both William and Dorothy were baptised, and where their father is laid to rest, walk along Market Place and within a few yards turn right up the narrow side street of Kirkgate. The church is almost opposite a small watering-hole, the Bitter End pub. Retrace your steps to Wordsworth House and the start of the William Wordsworth Way.

The River Derwent (the name is Celtic in origin, meaning 'clear running water') meanders through the town and passes behind Wordsworth House just beyond the garden wall. The river was seen by the poet in later years as having shaped his thoughts while still a babe-in-arms, and was the subject of a sonnet, *To the River Derwent*, and also a short extract in *The Prelude* (i.271–394).

The Derwent is around 33 miles long. It flows through two lakes, Derwent Water and Bassenthwaite Lake, and rises in the heartland of the Lake District, among the highest summits in England. To follow the Derwent to its birthplace, secreted in the heart of the Lakeland mountains, was one of the poet's childhood dreams; on the second day of this walk, that journey is partially completed.

In 1850 Cockermouth's All Saints Church was all but destroyed by fire. The reconstructed building fortunately includes the Wordsworth memorial window, which is immediately in front upon entering the churchyard through the iron gates. The grave of William's father is located over to the left of the window. Inside and to the left of the altar is a brass plaque celebrating the 'Glory of God and the memory of Wordsworth'.

>> To reach the youth hostel or campsite from Wordsworth House, cross Main Street and walk up Sullart Street and its continuation, Gallowbarrow. After about 350 yards turn right (signposted Egremont and Keswick), then immediately left (signposted Harris Park and Youth Hostel). Continue along Parkside Avenue to where this turns sharp right. Continue straight ahead following a stony track downhill to Double Mills.

At the bottom of the hill a footbridge spans the River Cocker. The youth hostel is in the old mill over to the right from the bridge; otherwise, continue for the Violet Bank campsite, a further ten minutes' walking, by crossing the river. At the far side of the bridge ignore the path left into Harris Park and the riverside route to the right, and instead walk forward up an embankment and slightly right into the residential estate.

Walk along Dale View, following this around a left-hand bend and then, after approximately 180 yards, turning right up Riverdale Drive. At the top of the hill turn right again at the T-junction, following Simonscales Lane for quarter of a mile. Shortly after leaving the housing estate turn left down the access drive to the campsite, the entrance of which is on the left after a further 350 yards.

TOWN CENTRE START

Where you spent the night will dictate which of the three possible starting points is yours. For those staying in town, use the directions as described above to reach the youth hostel, then follow instructions as if starting here, as below.

YOUTH HOSTEL START

Youth hostellers must cross the river bridge and turn right, along a level riverside footpath cutting across a wide meander loop of the Cocker. Around the bend the path soon passes beneath the A66 flyover (in late spring the banking here is carpeted with cowslips) and, after 450 yards, veers half left then right alongside a fence to reach and cross a stile by the

Simonscales Mill. The route from Violet Bank campsite descends the track on the left. Continue as below for Main Route Continuation.

CAMPSITE START

Campers may begin the walk by turning right out of the Violet Bank site, then left down the continuation of Simonscales Lane. A quarter of a mile after crossing the town bypass the old Simonscales Mill is reached by the River Cocker. The path from the town centre and youth hostel joins from the right. Go through the stile on the left just before the buildings. Continue as for Main Route Continuation.

MAIN ROUTE CONTINUATION

The first few miles criss-cross the predominantly lush farmland of Lorton Vale, providing easy, level going as a welcome precursor to the crossing of the Grasmoor Fells towards the day's end. From the stile by Simonscales Mill follow a footpath along the riverbank for three-quarters of a mile. Eventually the way takes to the top of a wooded banking overlooking the Cocker but very soon descends through a hedge on the right to reach a stile. Turn left and continue as far as Southwaite Bridge.

Turn left up the road and right at the next stile, along a footpath (signposted to Stanger). Almost immediately cross a footbridge and go forward, uphill slightly between thorn trees, and then follow a fence line across into the far corner of the field to find a stile. From there continue forward for almost a quarter of a mile, keeping to the right-hand edge of the field to enter a lane at a stile.

Cross the lane and the second stile opposite and walk straight forward along the right edge of the field to yet another stile after about 60 yards. Immediately in front is Stanger Farm. Cross the stile and turn left, picking up the farm access track and following this to the road. Turn right then right again at the first public footpath, taking a line indicated by the fingerpost, diagonally half left, aiming for the far corner of the meadow where a kissing gate will be found beside a mature oak.

Once through the gate, proceed parallel to a fence and negotiate another stile; then, maintaining the same line, go forward and over another stile in a hedgerow, and yet another a few yards ahead. From here cross the next pasture with a small wood to the left to reach a kissing gate in a hawthorn hedge. Beyond this our route becomes a bridleway, though this is not obvious, then the way becomes clear and is traced left through a gate in the corner a few yards distant. The hills flanking the east side of Lorton Vale now begin to dominate the forward view, a constant reminder that the hardest, and perhaps more satisfying, part of the day is yet to come. >>

Lorton Vale is a picturesque part of Cumbria extending for some seven miles south-east and southwards between Cockermouth and the expanse of Crummock Water. It presents a verdant prospect with only a scattering of tiny settlements amid a patchwork-like arrangement of dry-stone walled enclosures. The latter present a pleasing effect as a whole, rather like uncertain brushstrokes upon a rural canvas. The modest Fellbarrow (1,364 feet) flanks the vale to the west, its eastern side gradually rising in elevation south from the Whinlatter Pass, beginning with Dodd and peaking with the fine hill of Grasmoor, whose windswept head is raised 2,795 feet above sea-level.

>> From the gate proceed straight forward 100 yards or so ahead to a wall and a second gate. Ignore the latter and instead to its right cross the ladder stile and continue forward along the line of trees to reach and cross a stile in a fence at the far side of the pasture. Beyond this, and keeping to the same bearing, cross the next two pastures, eventually walking beside a hedgerow and crossing a short section of open pasture to reach the corner of a fence. Proceed alongside this for a further 40 yards or so before turning left over a stile to follow the path to a road.

Turn right along this into the sleepy village of Low Lorton (don't blink or you'll miss it!), picking up a path on the left (fingerpost) soon after the Wheatsheaf Inn. A few yards down the road is the famous Lorton Hall, historically linked with two British monarchs. Proceed along the path for the church, but just before this veer right then left around a house to enter and turn right along a lane. Within just a few yards turn left (fingerpost) through a gate. A path continues between two fences as far as another road.

Turn right here and amble through High Lorton, where our route now starts to gain height along the eastern flank of the valley. At the far end of the village turn left up a narrow lane for Boonbeck and Scales. Walk uphill for 70 yards, looking out for a fingerpost, and turn right here through a kissing gate and along a path beside a fence. This soon becomes a wall, but when this ends walk left towards a farm. Go through an iron gate here and walk up the farm track. Just around a left bend turn off to the right, go through a gate and continue uphill along a track which in summer becomes a green country lane coloured with wild blooms. >>

One of the more famous associations of the vale is centred upon the interesting Lorton Hall, a fortified building near Low Lorton incorporating a fine pele tower and some oak panelling. In the middle of the 11th century this part of the Lake District belonged to Scotland, and it was here that King Malcolm III, king from 1057, stayed overnight while touring what was then the kingdom of Strathclyde. It was here too in 1653 that King Charles II was entertained as the guest of the Lady of the Manor, Mary Winder. Readers who are intrigued by tales of things that go bump in the night might take note that the hall has a tradition of hauntings by a woman carrying a lighted candle.

Behind the village hall, known as Yew Tree Hall, once stood the famous yew tree of High Lorton written about by Words-worth, and celebrated in his poem *Yew Trees* which opened 'There is a Yew-tree, pride of Lorton Vale'. From beneath the spreading branches of this ancient evergreen the founder of the Quaker movement, George Fox, once preached his faith to a gathering flock.

>> High Swinside Farm is reached and passed on its left side, the walk continuing along a track to join the road. The main climb of the day now looms ever nearer. Turn right down the road and after about 200 yards turn left on a path taking off at a tangent just before a gate closing the road. Contour forward to locate a path running parallel with a wall seen immediately ahead. When a small brook is reached there is a parting of the ways, our route following the right-hand fork.

The path contours along and down to a ford over Hope Beck, beyond which the path keeps to the wall side. Apart from an initial boggy stretch the way ahead soon develops into a fine terrace walk. After nearly half a mile Cold Gill is forded; then, passing through a gate, the route contours once again, this time with a wall on the left. The path traverses beneath some stark rock outcrops with the forward view dominated by the flat-topped summit of Grasmoor, the loftiest point on this side of the valley.

I thoroughly enjoyed this section of the walk: I hadn't yet begun the main climb, and my gaze was distracted by splendid panoramas the length of the vale. In the distance away to the south of Crummock Water, a handful of mountains near the head of Ennerdale beckoned with alluring rocky crests, but I would have to wait almost two weeks before my weary feet carried me through those cloud-wreathed heights.

Two miles after departing from the road, a wall corner is finally reached where the way then takes off half left as a green swathe dividing the bracken-covered slopes. After gaining a spur, the path intersects another trail from right to left leading to the summit of Whiteside. Cross this and continue forward on a contouring path into Gasgale Gill, a narrow valley that slips impressively between the two hills of Whiteside and Grasmoor.

The route picks its way across scree, rock outcrops and heather-clad slopes. For two miles it traces the course of Liza Beck through terrain that has a distinctly isolated ambience, a sensation that imparts to the lone walker a feeling of vulnerability that is intensified when leaden clouds hang overhead. Don't despair, however. The trail at length gains the pass (Coledale Hause) while there is an ever-present chance of spotting buzzard or even peregrine falcon.

At the head of the pass well-defined paths are intersected heading left for Hopegill Head, home of the rare red alpine catchfly (*Lychnis viscaria*), and right for Crag Hill and Grasmoor. Our route, however, lies half right where a good trail begins its descent into lonely Coledale.

The footpath contours down beside Force Crag and its attendant disused mine, the only blemish in an otherwise beautiful vista. Just below the mine, a dirt track is joined and followed down the valley a further two miles and more, with the massive Blencathra beckoning in the distance. The village of Braithwaite comes into view and eventually the track joins the Winlatter Pass road on its western approach.

Turn right and walk down the road into Braithwaite. Continue through the village, ignoring the turn-off right for the youth centre in Coledale, and then where the road turns sharp left continue forward by the Ivy House Hotel, turning right immediately after this towards the bridge over the beck a few yards ahead. Turn left just before this (signposted Keswick). After 30 yards pick up the footpath signposted off to the right to reach the Cotgate campsite. >>

Like many Cumbrian villages Braithwaite was originally established in a forest clearing by Nordic settlers. It is located at the foot of Coledale a mere stone's throw from the entrance to the Newlands Valley. It was here in Braithwaite that the Cumberland Pencil Company was begun, but a fire in 1898 forced a move to nearby Keswick.

The village church is dedicated to St Herbert, the local saint who is said to have been the hermit on the island on Derwent Water featured in the Wordsworth poem, *For the Spot where the Hermitage Stood on St Herbert's Island, Derwent-Water*. Among the many Lakeland treasures once delved for in the vicinity, barytes (barium sulphate) was sought and extracted in quantity from the mine at the head of Coledale.

>> Those wishing to stay in Keswick's youth hostel or guest-houses should continue along the path skirting the perimeter of the large campsite, between this and a brook to reach the far corner of the site where a stile is crossed. Walk forward alongside the stream, crossing a footbridge after about 150 yards to continue on the opposite bank. At the bridge the shapely Grizedale Pike is seen rising immediately ahead.

Follow the stony track to a minor road at Little Braithwaite Farm. Turn left down this as far as another bridge. At the far side of this footpaths take off both left and right. Walkers intending to start Day 2 at Braithwaite by omitting Keswick centre or the two route options will turn right here to continue into Borrowdale (see next stage instructions).

If heading for Keswick, however, walkers must go left through a gate and cross the stile immediately on its right. Walk forward, keeping to the fence on your right, heading in the direction of Skiddaw mountain visible in the distance. In a little over a quarter of a mile go through a gate and another a yard or two beyond, then cross the main A66 or, instead, use the alternative and safer cattle creep beneath and to the left.

At the far side of the next pasture, cross a step stile and turn left over a bridge, then go immediately right along a driveway (public footpath). The way then takes off at a tangent through a gate within a few steps. Carry on straight forward taking a vague line slightly uphill which more or less follows a fence line forward and to the right.

Over a rise a track is intersected leading quickly to a stile by some houses. From here a metalled lane is followed downhill back to the main road. Cross this and walk left, then take the first right for Portinscale. In about 70 yards turn right along a private road (signposted public footpath) and follow this for about 250 yards. Look for a residence called Little Ellers and opposite this trace a path between a housing development to reach a road.

Turn right and then first left just after Dale Garth Hotel (fingerpost), at this point noting the curious Dorothy Well situated on the corner. Walk up the lane to where this splits and, taking the right fork, follow this to where it bends left. The way lies straight ahead beyond a step stile and down the field to the riverside.

Turn right at the bottom of the hill, over two stiles and forward through a manicured area beside the river to reach and cross the suspension bridge across the River Derwent. The path into Keswick town veers off right through a gate immediately beyond the river crossing. Obvious made-up field paths are from here then traced for half a mile to the outskirts of the town at the bridge over the River Greta.

Turn right here for the centre. To reach the youth hostel walk up Main Street to the Moot Hall information centre. Beyond this, bear left along Station Street and its continuation Station Road to the river bridge. The hostel is signposted down steps on the left here just before the river. >>

Practically the whole of modern Keswick has Victorian origins that grew in the wake of its mining heritage and the coming of the railway. The discovery of graphite was an important factor in its subsequent growth. At first used in the casting of cannonballs for the British Navy, its use rapidly developed into a major pencil manufacturing industry which still flourishes to this day, though local graphite is now no longer employed.

Keswick in Wordsworth's day was once little more than a scattered collection of cottages and the Moot Hall. Seen from afar, the most prominent buildings then, besides its meeting hall, were Greta Hall and the interesting church at Crosthwaite. The town's rural station was described as 'beauty, horror and immensity united' by Dr John Brown, while the writer, Gray, was 'wrapped in Elysium' with the six days he spent there.

Despite the mixed sentiments of its earlier visitors, such was the setting that Keswick attracted the most prominent people from the arts, including the famous poets of the romantic period, Southey, Shelley, Coleridge and, of course, Wordsworth.

The magnificent Moot Hall has a 17th-century vintage and was erected on the site of an earlier building dating from 1571 that had been used both as a courthouse and a prison. The town's roots extend much further back, to the Dark Ages, in fact, as is evidenced by the Anglo-Saxon place-name component *-wick* and the late Neolithic/early Bronze Age stone circle at nearby Castlerigg.

USEFUL INFORMATION

Accommodation: Ample choice of hotels, guest-houses and B&Bs in Braithwaite, Portinscale and Keswick.

Camping: Cotgate campsite, Braithwaite. Open summer. £2.70/night/person or £3.50 minimum. Full facilities plus shop and café. Tel: (017687) 78343.

Youth Hostel: Station Road, Keswick. Tel: (017687) 72484.

Transport: Bus service Nos. X5, 34, 35 linking Penrith with Whitehaven stops in Keswick and Cockermouth.

Supplies: Shop in Braithwaite. Good selection of shops etc in Keswick.

Refreshments: Several pubs and cafés in Keswick. Pub in Braithwaite.

Tourist Information: Moot Hall, Main Street, Keswick. Tel: (017687) 725758.

DAY 2
Keswick to Longthwaite

SUMMARY

Distance: 9 miles if starting at Braithwaite campsite or
Keswick centre. (If including the Applethwaite variation
add a further 6 miles for a Keswick start, 4 miles if
starting in Braithwaite.)

Total Ascent: 82 feet (25 metres).

Expected Duration: 3–6 hours depending on whether the
options are included.

Map: 1:25000 Outdoor Leisure Series sheet No.4.

Terrain and Difficulty: Delightful, easy walking mostly
through broadleaf woodlands, at times beside the lake
with glimpses of overshadowing crags and mountains.

Highlights: If starting in Keswick centre the route includes
the very fine 17th-century Moot Hall and many sites
connected with Wordsworth if the Applethwaite variation
is included.

Option: An ascent of Skiddaw (allow extra 2.5 hours).
Additional ascent, 2,844 feet (867 metres).

Keswick and its environs have a multitude of Wordsworthian
connections, making it a natural centre at which to terminate
the first day of this trail. The streets are kept meticulously
clean and it is an ideal springboard from which to explore the
surrounding countryside whether following the William
Wordsworth Way or not. There are a number of museums –
one features the cars of famous people and another recounts
the history of pencil manufacture. The town is popular with
summer visitors – indeed tourism is today its *raison d'être*.

Depending on your choice of accommodation, there are
several likely starting points for the second stage of this walk.
The route extends south, by the wooded lakeside and into the
delightfully craggy hollow of Borrowdale. This stage is
relatively short, but may be lengthened with the addition of
the Applethwaite Loop or the optional ascent of Skiddaw.

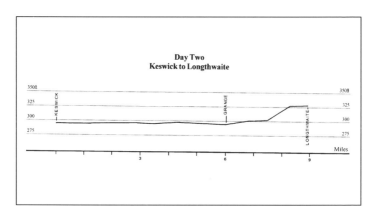

Day Two
Keswick to Longthwaite

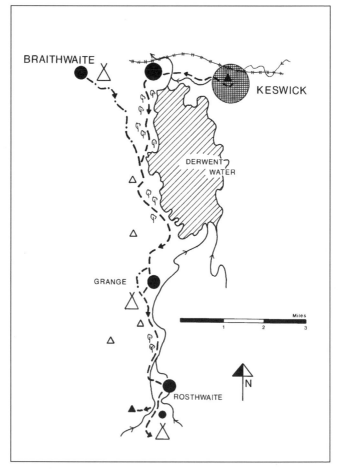

YOUTH HOSTEL START

At the top of the steps from the riverbank, turn right along Station Road and straight across into Station Street at the first junction. Bear right down Main Street beside the tourist information centre, housed in the magnificent Moot Hall, and from there follow directions as for the Keswick Town Centre Start below.

KESWICK TOWN CENTRE START

Starting outside the Moot Hall building, continue north-west out of town along Main Street (A5271) in the direction of Cockermouth. Where the road spans the River Greta it is just possible to glimpse Greta Hall on a low hilltop away through the trees to the right, behind the pencil factory and museum. >>

Greta Hall was built by one William Jackson, said by local tradition to have been the master of Benjamin in William's itinerary poem, *The Wagonner*. From 1800 the Hall was home to William's friend and fellow poet, Samuel Coleridge, until estrangement from his wife forced him to leave, and also to William's brother-in-law, Robert Southey, who moved in and remained there until his death in 1843. The poet Shelley also lodged here for a brief period after he had eloped with his young bride in 1811.

>> If omitting the Applethwaite Loop, take the public footpath for Portinscale at the far side of the road, on the left, immediately after crossing the bridge over the Greta. Follow this west for about half a mile across the fields to where a metalled path is met trending right to left for the suspension bridge over the River Derwent. After crossing the bridge follow directions as for Main Route South.

If taking in the Applethwaite Loop or intending to climb Skiddaw, continue from the bridge spanning the Greta down the A5271 for 400 yards to the junction with the Crosthwaite Road and Limepots Road, presided over by the Catholic church. Here carry straight on down the B5289 until the road swerves to the left. Take the turning right for Crosthwaite along a minor lane leading to a mini roundabout by St Kentigern's Church, which is straight in front. The churchyard here is the final resting place of Robert Southey (1774–1843). To continue from this point, follow directions as for Applethwaite Loop as below.

Skiddaw looms over Crosthwaite Church, near Keswick

Crosthwaite Church is a late Perpendicular edifice with some 14th-century fabric and, it is thought, 12th-century foundations. Tradition accords that St Kentigern erected a cross and preached here in the sixth century; indeed the name Crosthwaite implies in the old Norse a forest clearing in which a cross stood. The church has a few interesting features, including a 14th-century font and a marble monument (inside) to Robert Southey. An epitaph by William adorns the monument. Signs direct visitors to Southey's grave in the churchyard. He was installed as Poet Laureate in 1813, the same year William and his family moved from Grasmere to Rydal.

BRAITHWAITE START (INCLUDING **APPLETHWAITE LOOP**)
To continue the walk including either the Applethwaite Loop or Skiddaw options, pick up the footpath skirting around the south side of the campsite, between this and a stream, to reach the far corner of the site where a stile is crossed. Continue forward alongside the beck, crossing a footbridge after about 150 yards to proceed on the opposite bank.

Follow the stony track to a minor road at Little Braithwaite Farm. Turning left here you very soon reach a bridge, at the far side of which a footpath bears left through a gate and immediately right over a stile. Walk forward, keeping to the fence on your right, heading in the direction of Skiddaw seen in the distance. In a little over quarter of a mile, go through one gate and another a yard or two beyond, and cross the main road, or instead use the safer cattle creep to the left.

At the far side of the next pasture, cross a step stile and turn left over a bridge then immediately right along a driveway (signposted public footpath). Within a few steps veer off at a tangent through a gate and carry on forward, taking a vague line slightly uphill which more or less follows a fence line around to the right.

Over the rise a track is intersected leading quickly to a stile. Beyond this follow a metalled lane downhill to the main A66, cross this and walk left, then take the first right for Portin-scale. In about 70 yards turn right along a private road (signposted public footpath) and follow this for about 250 yards. Here turn left up a path opposite Little Ellers and follow this between a housing development to a road.

Turn right and just after Dale Garth Hotel turn left (finger-post). Note the curious Dorothy Well situated on this street corner. Walk up the lane to where this splits and, taking the right fork, follow this to where it bends left. The way lies straight ahead beyond a step stile and down the field to the riverside. Turn right at the bottom of the hill, climb over two stiles and continue forward beside the river through a land-scaped area to reach and cross the suspension bridge across the River Derwent.

Walk along the widening metalled path from the bridge to where it joins the B5289. Cross this and immediately turn left up a narrow leafy track (signposted Crosthwaite) which provides welcome shade on a hot day. After about 400 yards St Kentigern's Church, the oldest building in Keswick, is reached by a mini roundabout where a lane on the right comes from the B5289 and the town centre. To continue for Skiddaw or the Applethwaite Loop from the roundabout, follow instructions as below.

APPLETHWAITE LOOP

Leaving the roundabout by Crosthwaite Church, walk in a north-easterly direction, picking up a footpath heading uphill, between the school access road and tennis courts. Walking between fences, head for the left-hand extremity of the school building, where at the corner the main path turns sharp right.

Our continuation, part of the Allerdale Ramble, is through a kissing gate in front, and downhill half right to pass beneath a disused railway line. Follow the path forward, crossing the A66. Continue along a footpath signposted to Thrushwood, crossing a footbridge immediately followed by a ladder stile.

Following a bearing trending for the summit of Skiddaw, aim for the far corner of the meadow to find a stile and kissing gate. Ignore the gate in favour of an overgrown path beyond the stile which continues forward between hedges to reach and cross the A591. Go over the stile, head downhill and along a path keeping to a fence across pastures, through a gate and eventually passing on the left side of a barn.

The nearing bulk of Skiddaw now forms a magnificent backcloth to the hamlet of Applethwaite seen immediately ahead, while away to the right the white-painted buildings of Ormathwaite stand out in contrast to the overshadowing hill-sides. Still keeping to the fence, the path is traced for a further quarter-mile, then heads left around a corner to reach a gate. Go through this and follow another pathway, often over-grown with nettles (shorts wearers beware!), between hedges, uphill to a second gate at the outskirts of Applethwaite. Turn left through a watersplash and right to enter the hamlet.

Walk up the road, passing a turning to the left (departure point for the optional ascent of Skiddaw: see directions below), and take the left fork when the way ahead shortly splits. Continue uphill between a row of cottages and the stream to the road junction at the head of the hamlet. The property seen immediately in front, up alongside the continuation of Applethwaite Gill, was once owned by Words-worth, known then as Gill and today called Ghyll. >>

The property at Applethwaite was a gift from the poet's good friend Sir George Beaumont, a noted landscape painter and art patron of the day. Although William never lived here, he was undoubtedly grateful for this act of generosity for it made him a freeholder of the county of Cumberland with the added right to vote. The gift, honoured in the verse *At Applethwaite, Near Keswick*, had been one of many well-meaning attempts by friends to bring Wordsworth and Coleridge closer together. In the event this never happened.

>> Turn right along the road and immediately right again,

back downhill to the point of entry into the hamlet just beyond Field View House. Turn left here across the ford and over the left hand of the two stiles (for Underscar). Cross two more stiles and proceed forward to a kissing gate. This is a public right of way though no footpath is visible on the ground. From the gate strike across a meadow towards some buildings just visible beyond the rise. Cross a footbridge and go through a gate. Walk along by a hedge, beyond which can be seen Ormathwaite House, home of William's friend and benefactor, Raisley Calvert.

A few yards along the hedge pass through the gate on the left and turn right along the lane, then right at the road junction to pick up a footpath on the left after 180 yards. Follow the obvious farm track. Continue through a kissing gate and aim for a stile where a small stream is crossed. Bear right here along the fence to a gate. Don't go through the latter, but instead walk left along the fence side as indicated by the direction arrows.

As you top the rise, the footpath veers slightly left alongside a fence to the left of the house to a find a kissing gate leading onto a bridleway where the Cumbria Way descends from Skiddaw. Turn right here, cross the bridge over the A66 and at the junction turn left along Briar Rigg. About 200 yards later take the lane leading off to the left. A bend is reached after maybe quarter of a mile where a left branch leads to Windebrowe, a house nestling beneath the slopes of Latrigg that has connections with Wordsworth. At the bend turn right along a footpath then left to cross the River Greta by way of a fine, single-arched bridge to meet the A591. >>

Windebrowe, originally called Windy Brow, was the farmhouse home of the local Calvert family. It was here in the springtime of 1794 that William and his sister Dorothy stayed; and where later that same year William nursed his dying friend, Raisley. The house is not normally open to the public though a viewing of the rooms where the Wordsworths stayed can sometimes be secured by prior arrangement. The river was the subject of a sonnet, *To the River Greta, Near Keswick*, in which Wordsworth likened its boulder-rolling character to the River Cocytus in Hades.

>> Turn right along the A591 and follow this the half-mile into town or, easier on booted feet, within a few yards gain access to a permissive footpath along the disused railway

embankment by climbing the steps behind the filling station. Turn right (west) along the railway trackbed, over the main road and the river, then after 180 yards leave the path by the Keswick Timeshare Information Office, turning sharp left beneath the old railway and walking along the road passing the Keswick Country House Hotel to a T-junction.

Turn left along Station Road between Upper and Lower Fitz Parks and, walking past the Keswick Museum and Art Gallery, cross the River Greta. The youth hostel is situated down a flight of steps on the right and along the riverbank immediately after crossing the bridge. Continue through the town using directions as for Youth Hostel Start, as far as the suspension bridge over the River Derwent, and from there continue as for Main Route South.

ASCENT OF SKIDDAW (OPTIONAL)

This may be taken in as a variation at the beginning of this stage if desired, though it is a steep climb and will entail an ascent of 2,844 feet and add a further 2.5 hours or so to the total journey time. >>

Skiddaw played a prominent role in the life of William Wordsworth. As a young boy he often contemplated the profile of the distant hill from his home town of Cockermouth. It features in his poem *The Wagonner*. He owned land overshadowed by the mountain, which must have been in his thoughts many times when visiting friends in Keswick. In 1815 his brother-in-law and fellow poet, Robert Southey, organised a great gathering on the barren summit of Skiddaw to celebrate the Duke of Wellington's victory at the Battle of Waterloo. Here they held a magnificent feast and bonfire attended by the Southeys, Dorothy Wordsworth, William and his wife, Mary, as well as numerous servants and hangers-on.

>> Follow the Applethwaite Loop directions from Keswick as far as the quiet hamlet of Applethwaite, and from the T-junction at its centre walk west along the lane to Mill Beck for approximately 200 yards. Here bear left between a house and two garages to cross a stile and make a beeline for a gate at the far side of the field. From here walk above a wood to reach a kissing gate.

From here continue straight forward, the way indicated by occasional white marker arrows, passing behind a farmhouse and crossing a small footbridge here to reach another kissing gate. After passing through this, maintain the same line to yet a third kissing gate; then, following a hedge, bear right to pass a building on its left side. Continue with a fence on your left to a gate where a short section of walled lane is entered before passing to the right of a large shed (yellow arrows) to reach a lane at Mill Beck.

Turn right into the hamlet then left at the T-junction, crossing the bridge and walking along the lane. Just at the outskirts of Mill Beck turn sharp right up a track and through two gates. Trace the footpath for Skiddaw uphill, climbing steeply up the spur known as Stoups. After crossing a broken-down wall the gradient eases momentarily where the route threads its way through some marble outcrops. Beyond this, however, the path resumes its relentless angle.

The continuing stony path, coincident with the Allerdale Ramble, rises across the precipitous, heather-clad slopes giving superb views back across Keswick, Derwent Water and beyond to the hills flanking Borrowdale. Eventually arriving at the rounded summit of Carl Side, the continuing cairned path descends north-east to a wide saddle, and from here takes the obvious trail straight ahead, cutting up through scree slopes on the mountain's exposed western flank.

After a steep climb, a cairn marks where the main pathway is eventually met from the subsidiary summit of Little Man and from Keswick. Turn left along this, following the ridge to reach the main summit (3,054 feet) in little more than quarter of a mile. Return to Applethwaite by retracing the outward route. When returning along the ridge from the summit in mist take care to not overshoot the cairn marking where the path takes off to the right. To reach Keswick and continue the walk south into Borrowdale follow the instructions to Ormathwaite from the watersplash in Applethwaite hamlet, as described in Applethwaite Loop (see above).

BRAITHWAITE START (WITHOUT **APPLETHWAITE LOOP**)
From Cotgate campsite follow instructions as if including the Applethwaite Loop (see directions above) as far as the bridge just beyond Little Braithwaite Farm. Turn right through a kissing gate here and along a footpath tracing the true left bank of Newlands Beck. Ahead can be seen the peak of Dale Head rising in the distance, with Cat Bells and Maiden Moor on the left.

The path offers excellent views of the Newlands Valley, and is an ideal place to find wild flowers, including several species of vetch, stitchwort, foxglove, speedwell and campion. On a balmy summer's day it is one of those places that make walking in the Lakes a memory to treasure.

After about three-quarters of a mile a bridge is met complete with a few stalactites clinging to the underside of its single span. Ignore the bridge and continue along the banking for 150 yards to reach a gate and stile. Ignore the path over the latter and instead walk forward through the gate, tracing the fence around to the left, before striking across the field, at the far side of which the continuation is found along a narrow, hedged lane to a gate.

Go through this and uphill to a road. Turn left and walk past Swineside Inn and the turning for Braithwaite, continuing along a minor road giving a fine panorama of the Newlands Valley. Proceed to a junction after a quarter-mile, taking the right branch (signposted Grange) down the hill. Immediately after the Swineside Lodge Hotel walk uphill to the right. The minor but curiously named hill of Cat Bells rears up in front with Causey Pike obvious across the dale to the right. >>

It was in the Newlands Valley that immigrant German miners delved for copper, silver and gold. Mrs Tiggy-Winkle in Beatrix Potter's children's stories also had her home here and had many an adventure on neighbouring Cat Bells, a gentle hill whose name is probably a corruption of Cat Bield.

>> Soon the walker will come to a hairpin bend on a hill. Turn down a woodland path to the left (signposted for Keswick, Brandelhow and Hawes End launch pier). The metalled lane is soon reached by the entrance to Derwent Bay Woodcrafts Centre. To continue, turn right here and as for Main Route South (see below) follow the directions from this point.

MAIN ROUTE SOUTH

After crossing the suspension bridge over the Derwent continue up the road to a junction and turn left through a residential district, following the road to a double bend after about half a mile. Just beyond the bends take a public road off to the left to Nichol Point.

At the boathouse follow a rising footpath on the right of the buildings, crossing a metalled lane and continuing straight on along a track (signposted footpath). A quarter of a mile later the way is joined by a footpath from the right, and a few yards further it reaches the gate to Langholme House. The path carries on forward to the right of this (signposted Cat Bells) and continues between fences with hills appearing between the trees ahead.

A clearing is crossed to a footbridge, beyond which the path rises slightly, enters the woods again and before long meets a road by the entrance to the Derwent Bay Woodcrafts Centre. Continue along the lane for a little way (footpath signposted to lake shore and Manesty), then after a few yards look for the yellow direction arrows by Hawes End, indicating a footpath to the left along a dirt track. About 60 yards later ignore the path going left (lake shore and Manesty) to continue straight ahead for Brandelhow Wood.

At Hows End Cottage Centre bear right along a fence line, cross two stiles, then head off along a woodland trail from where St Herbert's Island can be seen. Pass a barn, ignoring the stiles on the right just before and after it, to reach a gate. Go through this and walk along a track through pleasant mixed woodlands.

Ford a couple of small brooks before rising up a banking and then veering left along a more obvious track, soon curving to the left and down another banking. At the foot of the slope cross a track intersecting at right-angles and carry on forward, the way soon descending towards the lake and sweeping past the landing stage just before Brandelhow Bay. >>

After Windermere, Keswick's own lake is perhaps the most popular in the Lake District. It is also one of the shallowest, making it among the first to freeze over in the grip of winter. One of the largest islands, that named after St Herbert, is said to have been where the saint had his hermitage. In 1565, during its mining heyday, Keswick received an influx of specialist German miners, referred to earlier, who subsequently established their own colony on nearby Derwent Island.

The first acquisitions of the National Trust in the Lake District embraced the woods at Brandelhow Park, very soon followed by land at Gowbarrow, along the shores of Ullswater. The Trust later increased its holdings to the point where today it is the largest landowner in the district. Nearby Brackenburn is famous as the former home of Sir Hugh Walpole (1884–1941), novelist and author of the 'Herries'

novels, many of the settings for his stories being identifiable as places here in Borrowdale.

>> The way veers up to the right, as a stony path leading to a gate, but the main route takes off to the left, up a few stone steps, then straight forward through a gate. Turn left and follow a fence down a steep banking and forward towards Brandelhow Cottage, passing this on its left-hand side to reach and pass through a kissing gate.

Early morning view of Skiddaw, seen across Derwent Water from Abbot's Bay

Follow a broad track into Rupert's Wood for 30 yards to a fork and, keeping to the right, pick up a footpath (signposted Lodore) on the left opposite a cottage, The Warren. This traces an obvious trail into the woodlands of Manesty Park. Very soon there are good views across Derwent Water to Skiddaw and Blencathra from Abbot's Bay and nearby Myrtle Bay.

About five minutes' walking from The Warren a banking covered in tree roots is reached where several ways diverge.

Keeping to the path nearest the shoreline, follow this around the fringe of Myrtle Bay and through a gate in a wall. Continue forward through more open country colonised by bracken and silver birch. Castle Crag stands prominent in the long view up the valley.

Some 30 yards beyond the gate the path becomes a raised wooden walkway which allows walkers a dry crossing of meadows frequently inundated by floodwaters. Look for the spotted marsh orchid (*Dactylorhiza purpurella*), the yellow flowers of bog asphodel (*Narthecium ossifragum*) and at least two species of the curious sundew, a fly-eating plant of the Drosera family. After prolonged rainfall the famous Falls of Lodore can be seen tumbling through the woods backing the Lodore Swiss Hotel just across the valley. Away to its right the bare 'head' of Gowder Crag protrudes menacingly from the trees covering the valley side. >>

Though the Lodore Falls won universal acclaim long before Wordsworth's day, their beauty and scale provided him with lines for his poem, *An Evening Walk*. Overshadowing both the falls and the Swiss Hotel, an outcrop of Skiddaw slates (deposited *c*.500–450 million years ago as muddy sediments in

Borrowdale with the wooded Castle Crag rising left of centre

a shallow sea) rises from the forested slopes. Gowder Crag was the place where a 'blooming lass' extracted peat as described in the poem *Epistle to Sir G.H. Beaumont*.

>> At the end of the second and longer boardwalk, ignore the third one and instead bear to the right along a path through bracken and head for a wall at the edge of the wood. Ignore a gate here to trace a path left alongside the wall to just beyond a corner where a second gate is found. Up ahead the village of Grange comes into view. Go through the kissing gate here and yet a third one a few yards further on. After five minutes' walking, you will reach the valley road; turn left and proceed as far as the Borrowdale Gate Hotel.

If you wish to stop for refreshments, continue into the village, otherwise follow directions as for Southern Continuation (Grange Bypass), as below. Walk past the chapel to find the café about 70 yards beyond, at the last bend before the river. To leave the village and continue for Rosthwaite, walk back towards the chapel, but just before this, on the left, turn up a metalled lane (signposted public bridleway Rosthwaite, Seatoller and Honister).

Follow the bridleway for approximately quarter of a mile until, shortly after entering the National Trust Hollows Farm property (sign) at a gate, the lane bends to the right. At this point Castle Crag is visible just ahead. Immediately around the bend turn left on a dirt track branching off for Hollows Farm campsite. At this point the Grange bypass joins from Hollows Farm. Continue by following the directions as below.

The village of Grange derives its name from the fact that it was once a monastic outstation managed by the lay brothers of Furness Abbey in the 12th century. It featured also in the 'Herries' stories by Sir Hugh Walpole. Many years ago a cave at Castle Crag was the summer 'home' of self-styled adventurer Millican Dalton, known locally as the Professor of Adventure.

SOUTHERN CONTINUATION (GRANGE BYPASS)

To bypass Grange pick up a footpath (fingerpost) opposite the Borrowdale Gate Hotel, just on the north side of the village, and trace a path skirting Grange on its west side. The rising path gives good views across the village. Soon a gate is reached, beyond which a track is met rising forward uphill. Turn left instead and walk down the track through Hollows

Farm and on down the lane to a junction where the bridleway route from Grange is joined. >>

Along with the river, the route is now squeezed into a narrowing of the valley known in the past as the 'Jaws of Borrowdale'. I always find walking through natural woodland good for the thought process, enabling me to daydream, to imagine other places, another age, the earth in the throes of its primordial birth. In my mind's eye Castle Crag soars out of the trees like some lost Inca fortress that is being reclaimed by the encroaching tropical jungle. Being among trees is like being at one with nature, and Borrowdale is no exception; it is a place to dwell and which should be savoured, not rushed.

>> Turn right here along a walled lane leading to the campsite (the walls end after approximately quarter of a mile). Continue forward towards a sweeping bend in the River Derwent, just beyond which an obvious broad path continues straight forward.

Bear left on a path (signposted Rosthwaite) leading up the banking and quickly reaching a gate. Go through this, following the route through Long Hows Wood, at times overlooking the Derwent. The path climbs through a gap in a wall and rises over a hill to a fork. Turn left downhill passing a disused slate quarry beneath Castle Crag.

About 20 minutes' walk beyond the quarry cross the river bridge and turn right to follow a stony track into Rosthwaite. Walkers intending to stay at the camping barn, guest-house accommodation or inn should walk straight forward passing Yew Tree Farm. The bunkhouse is reached by continuing along to the T-junction by the village store, turning left here then right along the access to Hazelbank Country House (signposted to Stonethwaite and Watendlath). Once over the bridge turn left (signposted bridleway Watendlath) and through the gate immediately ahead where the barn is seen just on the right. >>

Rosthwaite is a picturesque walkers' village whose name belies its Nordic foundation. It was from here in 1818 that Dorothy Wordsworth made her remarkable ascent of Scafell Pike accompanied by her good friend, Miss Mary Barker. Six years earlier Dorothy had accompanied William on a walking tour when they stayed in Rosthwaite. The nearby Johnny Wood, backing onto the Longthwaite youth hostel, displays typical oak woodlands owned by the National Trust and now protected as an SSSI (Site of Special Scientific Interest).

>> To continue to the campsite and youth hostel at Longthwaite turn right immediately after Yew Tree Farm, following the way around the back of the farm. After about 100 yards turn right between buildings and find a footpath (fingerpost) turning left through a gate. Proceed along the wall side to cross a stile at the far side of the paddock.

Beyond this veer half right, go through a gate and turn left, heading for a cottage. Go through a stile and gate here to reach the metalled lane. The youth hostel is a few minutes' walk down this to the right, located on the edge of woodland on the far bank of the river. To continue for the campsite walk straight forward along the lane, then turn right through a gap stile on the left-hand bend.

A narrow path, continuing between a wall and hedge, leads in a few yards to a second stile over which the path carries straight on forward, up a wooded banking and along its crest to the far side of the field. Here find and cross a ladder stile, go forward to a gate in the far wall, and from here turn left down the road. The campsite is on the right within a few yards.

USEFUL INFORMATION

Accommodation: Several B&Bs in Rosthwaite and Longthwaite.

Bunkbarn: Dinah Hoggus camping barn, Rosthwaite. Open all year. £3/night/person. Tel: (017687) 77237.

Camping: Chapel Farm campsite, Longthwaite. Open all year. £2.50/night/person. Showers, WC and sinks. Enquiries to Gillercombe Guest-house. Tel: (017687) 77602.

Youth Hostel: Longthwaite Hostel. Tel: (017687) 77257.

Transport: Bus service Nos.77 and 77A link Keswick with Buttermere via Grange Bridge and Seatoller. Seatoller is also served by No.79 from Keswick via Grange Bridge and Rosthwaite.

Supplies: Shop in Rosthwaite.

Refreshments: Pub in Rosthwaite. Grange Bridge Café in Grange. Open until 7.30 p.m. daily.

Tourist Information: Seatoller Barn. Tel: (017687) 77294.

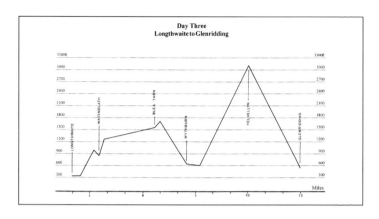

**Day Three
Longthwaite to Glenridding**

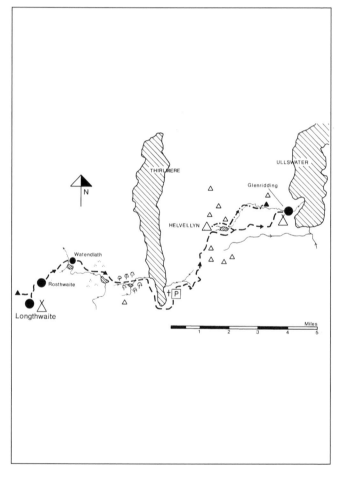

DAY 3
Longthwaite to Glenridding

SUMMARY
Distance: 13 miles (add 1 mile to YHA hostel).
Total Ascent: 4,117 feet (1,255 metres).
Expected Duration: Allow 6–7 hours.
Map: 1:25000 Outdoor Leisure Series sheet Nos.4 and 5.
Terrain and Difficulty: This stage crosses exposed fellsides and the highest point of the walk, on Helvellyn, at 3,116 feet (905m). The descent offers the choice of a stimulating crossing of Striding Edge, or a variation taking in the less exposed Swirrel Edge. This stage should not be attempted if storms are threatening or in poor visibility if you are less than confident in your navigation skills.
Highlights: Stunning mountain scenery.
Option: None.

To continue from the campsite in Longthwaite, retrace the steps of the previous day across the field paths (at this point coincident with Wainwright's Coast to Coast Walk) back into Rosthwaite at the junction by Yew Tree Farm. Follow the directions as in the previous section for the camping barn, but at the gate by the latter turn to the right and follow a stony path leading uphill. Very shortly a gate is reached beyond which the gradient increases with determination to a second gate.

Here a footpath departs off to the right for Stonethwaite, but our route, left, continues uphill passing through two more gates. At the second one carry straight on, ignoring a stile over to the right. Easy, level walking follows a broad pathway before the path loses height once again, down to the lake shore at Watendlath. Cross the packhorse bridge over Watendlath Beck. There is a welcome teashop immediately across from the bridge.

To continue for Wythburn turn left after crossing the stream, then right, around the back of a barn and walk up the road for 25 yards. Just before the carpark turn left between a wall and the stream and follow the path through a gate and on up the hillside. The trail out of Watendlath has been cleverly restored using natural materials by national park workers, giving a durable paved way zigzagging its way uphill towards a group of conifers.

The steep climb ends where the bridleway reaches a wall corner. Turning south here (signposted Wythburn and Blea Tarn) it then proceeds beside the wall with Watendlath Tarn immediately below and to the right. Far beyond this the mountain vista includes Honister Pass, Dale Head and, left from there, the central fells dominated not by the highest ground of the Scafells but by the obvious, steel-grey dome of Great Gable.

After contouring along the wall a cairned route is eventually picked up and for nearly two miles traced to Blea Tarn. This is one of several mountain lakes sharing this name, a more famous one featuring in the walk four days from now. The route to Blea Tarn crosses some poorly drained ground that after prolonged rain will necessitate the use of gaiters.

From the tarn a gradually ascending line soon reaches the watershed (2,013 feet), here marked by a fence line, where the Helvellyn range comes into view in all its majesty. The western skyline extends from the Dodds at the extreme left, over Helvellyn, Nethermost Pike, Dollywaggon Pike and south-wards to noble Fairfield. The point also commands excellent retrospective views.

Go through the gate in the fence and follow the route (cairned) heading down through bracken-covered slopes for the forest seen below. There seems to be various options for paths, but all converge upon the deer fence where a gate leads the way into the trees. Follow a woodland trail (cairned in places) downhill, across a short boardwalk, then descend a steep banking towards a stream heard below.

The bridleway merges eventually with a broad forest track. Continue straight forward along this until a junction with another track is reached and then turn right. Proceed downhill passing the secretive Harrop Tarn on your right to cross its outlet at a ford. At the far side follow a footpath to the left (signposted Wythburn) and continue for a few hundred yards to a ladder stile where the forest is left behind.

Turn left beyond the stile, along an increasingly rocky route

The William Wordsworth Way passes through the hamlet of Watendlath

that wends its way down beside the forest. When the bridleway swings right at a cairn, take the footpath departing left, tracing the steep line down to a gate. Pass through this and a second one a few yards beyond to reach the Armboth road.

Cross this and go through a gate to follow a pleasant path through Water Authority woodlands that flank the lake shore south-east for maybe half a mile, rejoining the road at the carpark by Stockhow Bridge. Turn left along the road to the T-junction with the A591. Cross this and turn left through a gate to follow a footpath (signposted Wythburn Church) contouring along parallel to and above the road for a half mile.

When Thirlmere comes into view the path merges with a forestry track (at the time of writing logging was taking place here and the way forward was haphazardly marked with posts). Still maintaining a course parallel to the road continue until the path meets the access track to Wythburn Church. Turn right up this into the carpark, where at the far side a gate leads onto the main bridleway route for Helvellyn. >>

The Reverend Joseph Sympson, a one-time close friend of Wordsworth, was the chaplain at the ancient Wythburn Church according to the poem *The Wagonner*, at Wytheburn's modest 'House of Prayer'. At the opposite side of the road once stood the Nag's Head, an inn popular with 19th-century travellers over the Raise. A few yards away from the church is a stone slab, a memorial to Matthew Arnold (1822–88) commemorating two walks over the Armboth Fells which inspired his verse, *Resignation.*

Thirlmere was originally two lakes until legislation was passed in 1879 allowing Manchester City Corporation to raise the water level by over 50 feet, creating one large reservoir. Among the casualties of the subsequent flooding were the old road, the hamlets of Armboth and Wythburn mentioned by Wordsworth, and a causeway bridge between the two lakes that was a popular meeting-place for William and Samuel Coleridge. On one occasion following a picnic near by, William, Dorothy, John Wordsworth, Coleridge and the Hutchinson sisters, Mary and Sarah, carved their names on a boulder, which subsequently become known as the Rock of Names. The boulder broke up during attempts to rescue it from the inundation.

>> Turn right here and for the first quarter-mile or so climb steeply up through the trees, crossing a logging track eventually to reach a gate where the path emerges into more open country. The path winds up the bracken-covered flanks, for a while running adjacent to the forest. Then, when this is finally left behind, the trail climbs into the crag-ringed head-waters of Comb Gill.

Above Comb Crags the gradient eases momentarily but unfortunately it soon resumes its relentless climb towards the third-highest summit in England. At the 2,620-feet (800-metres) contour the broad path becomes easier as it extends across the western slopes of Nethermost Pike. With the mind less focused upon gradients there is now time to enjoy backward glances across to the central fells, and the Furness Fells beyond.

Very soon the way reaches a cairn where a path from Nethermost Pike joins from the right, here overlooking Nethermost Cove, one of several crag-bound hollows that fall away precipitously into Grizedale. Follow the path upwards to the left along the brink of Lad Crag to reach the wind shelter. The true summit of Helvellyn lies a further 150 yards beyond this to the north. >>

Apart from the superb views obtained by standing on it, the summit of Helvellyn is somewhat featureless, and the ascent from Wythburn tedious. Its true character is revealed only when approaching from Grizedale or Greenside, when its east and north-east aspects form an impressive miscellany of crags underpinned by narrow spurs, features that will become apparent on the seventh day of this walk.

Indeed, the most dramatic aspect of Helvellyn, Striding Edge, is a fine airy crest which, along with the Swirrel Edge to the north, form two arms of a cove enclosing the secluded Red Tarn. The prospect east from the summit shelter is superb, and includes a bird's-eye view straight down into this sparkling Lakeland jewel, with Ullswater winding away to the far north-eastern horizon.

Continuing southwards along that notched skyline is the High Street range, which leads the eye naturally towards a knot of peaks forming the Kentmere mountains. Northwards from Helvellyn a range of more rounded summits, comprising Raise and the Dodds beyond that, stretch away towards Threlkeld like a rural roller-coaster.

Helvellyn is the highest point along an eight-mile range forming the watershed between Wythburn and its extension, St John's Vale, and Matterdale and the side valleys draining into Ullswater. William most frequently climbed Helvellyn, often accompanied by Dorothy, either bound for Keswick when visiting Coleridge or Southey, or when calling on friends and relations in Patterdale. It featured in several of his poems.

In 1799 he took Coleridge on a grand walking tour of the Lakes that included the summit of this popular mountain, and in 1805 an ascent was made by the poet, together with Sir Walter Scott and the chemist Humphrey Davy, via Striding Edge from Patterdale. Brownrigg Well, a spring located almost half a mile due west of the summit, was the site of William's 'Fountain of Mists'.

Helvellyn is without doubt the tourists' mountain and

probably the most visited in the Lake District if not the whole of England; on almost any summer weekend it is not uncommon for as many as 1,000 people to pay its wind-swept plateau a visit. Busy maybe, and famous without doubt, but not solely for its poetic links, for it was here that an Avro Alpha became the first aircraft to land on a mountain, and survive the manœuvre to take off again! This amazing feat was performed by John Leeming and the famous Australian pioneer aviator, Bert Hinkler (1892–1933), on 22 December 1926. A plaque honouring the fact is situated just a few feet south from the summit windbreak. Hinkler was killed in the Alps a few years later in an attempted record flight from Britain to Australia.

>> Once at the top of Helvellyn, the choice of descent route will ultimately be decided by the final destination of the day. Walkers may opt for either Striding Edge or Swirrel Edge if heading for the campsite, bunkbarn or hotels and guest-houses in Glenridding itself, or if in need of supplies, but Swirrel Edge is more convenient when the youth hostel or bothy at Greenside marks the end of the day.

STRIDING EDGE ROUTE

About 250 yards south-east (120 degrees) of the summit shelter, the Gough Memorial cairn stands at the point where Striding Edge butts up against the broad plateau forming the top, and where the path leading to its start can be found. The route along this airy crest, and its continuation along Bleaberry Crags, presents no great objective difficulties, though walkers of a nervous disposition may prefer to bypass the scrambly bits by taking an easier line at a slightly lower level.

About one and a quarter miles from the summit a wall will at length be met at a stile, a point indicated on Ordnance Survey maps as the Hole in the Wall. Ignore the stile here, and instead walk left, down the banking and follow the wall around a corner to find a second (ladder) stile. This is where the path meets that coming from Swirrel Edge.

SWIRREL EDGE ROUTE

For the continuation to Glenridding, Swirrel Edge provides a less intimidating alternative to its more infamous neighbour, but it is also a more convenient route for those walkers heading for Greenside. This fine ridge can be gained by walking north from the trig point (triangulation station) marking the true summit, and then at a cairn approximately 80 yards distant taking a way veering to the right (north-west) that picks its way down through outcrops of frost-shattered rock.

The route along this arête presents no problems, and shortly after the rocky bits end the way then splits, one way striking off for the summit of Catstye Cam, while our route descends towards the outfall of Red Tarn. Cross the outlet stream and continue straight ahead along a path trending east, gently climbing towards the Hole in the Wall and the ladder stile mentioned above, where the path from Striding Edge joins from the right. To reach the campsite and bunkhouse from this point, follow directions as for Continuation for Glenridding, otherwise see below for the alternative route to Greenside.

The secluded haven of Red Tarn has also known tragedy. An angler by the name of Charles Gough fell to his death from Striding Edge in April 1805 and his dog, a terrier, stood guard by his sorry remains a full three months. The story moved both Scott and Wordsworth to verse, the latter penning *Fidelity*, a poem telling of the faithful hound keeping its lonely vigil by its master's decaying corpse.

CONTINUATION FOR GREENSIDE

Take the obvious, broad pathway leading off on the north side of Red Tarn Beck near the lake outlet. This is traced around and across the eastern flank of Catstye Cam, then zigzags steeply down beside Red Tarn Beck before crossing the latter and, with an easier gradient, following its true right bank for about half a mile dominated by Sheffield Pike, seen in the forward view.

At this point the path splits, just above a small weir. Take the branch doubling back on itself to the left, cross the footbridge and continue into Greenside. This hamlet is formed from a group of former mining cottages that appear just ahead, and which seem to sit uncomfortably at the head of what at one time must have been a site of some beauty. Now, however, a huge, menacing spoil heap towers immediately above them, on the flanks of Sheffield Pike.

When a junction with an old mine track is reached (the route to Sticks Pass) the Swirrel bothy is just in front. To reach the youth hostel walk downhill to the right of this, passing the

Greenside Bury Jubilee Outdoor Pursuits Centre to reach a gate and bridge. Beyond these head off down the valley for about 150 yards, the youth hostel being found on the right just on the outskirts of the hamlet.

CONTINUATION FOR GLENRIDDING

At the Hole in the Wall do not cross the ladder stile but instead follow an obvious path along the left side of the wall rising towards Birkhouse Moor. When a cairn is reached by another wall corner, vacate the wall side route in favour of a newer line that very soon starts to wind steeply downhill towards Little Cove. This gives good views north towards Raise and the Dodds and, to the right of the large mine spoil heap at Greenside, the heights of Sheffield Pike.

The path eventually converges on the wall once again but the partnership is short-lived since the way then turns downhill to the left through Little Cove. After half a mile the way fords a stream by a small wood, then negotiates a rise to a stony track at a gate and ladder stile. Cross the latter and follow the path down to where it intersects another track by a cottage.

Walk left to another stile and proceed straight forward to where the track bends right. Immediately in front is Gillside Farm where walkers must seek permission to camp or use the bunkhouse. From the farm entrance walk down towards the bridge. The bunkhouse is situated on the left just before the latter, and the way into the campsite along a bridleway to the right (signposted to the carpark). Walkers planning to stay in a hotel or guest-house in Glenridding should follow the leafy bridleway through the campsite and down into the village, along the way ignoring a path off to the right signposted to Lanty's Tarn and Helvellyn.

In 1927 a dam serving the Greenside mines, and located at Keppel Cove to the north of Swirrel Edge, burst during severe storms. Floodwaters surged through Glenridding carrying away everything in its path, including trees and bridges, flooding many farms and houses in the village. Afterwards it was said that domestic flotsam, dead sheep and even a tea cabin were washed to the far shore of Ullswater.

USEFUL INFORMATION

Accommodation: Hotels and guest-houses in Glenridding.

Bunk Barn: A modern self-catering bunkhouse is sited adjacent to Gillside Farm, Glenridding. Open March to mid-November. Fee £6/night/person. Advance booking essential. Tel: (017684) 82346.

Bothy: Swirrel Bothy, Greenside. Tel: (017687) 72803.

Camping: At Gillside Farm, Glenridding. Full facilities with farm produce available at house. Open March to mid-November. £4/night/person plus £1 for tent. Tel: (017684) 82346.

Youth Hostel: Greenside hostel, Glenridding. Tel: (017684) 82269.

Transport: Bus service No.555 (Lakeslink) from Keswick to Windermere stops at Wythburn Church. Service No.37 between Patterdale and Workington stops at Glenridding, Threlkeld, Keswick and Cockermouth. Service No.108 links Penrith with Patterdale serving Yanwath Cottages, Pooley Bridge, Gowbarrow Cottages, Park Brow Foot and Glenridding.

Supplies: Shops in Glenridding. Gear shop selling camping gas.

Refreshments: Cafés in Watendlath and Glenridding.

Tourist Information: Beckside Carpark, Glenridding. Tel: (017684) 82414.

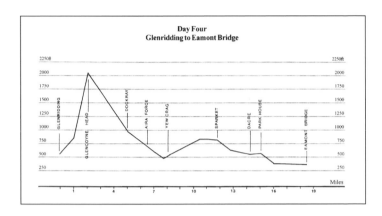

Day Four
Glenridding to Eamont Bridge

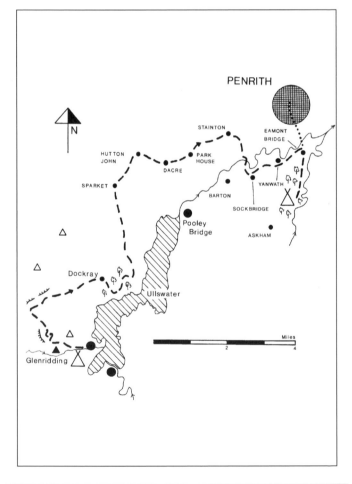

PENRITH

STAINTON

EAMONT
BRIDGE

HUTTON
JOHN

PARK
HOUSE

DACRE

YANWATH

SPARKET

BARTON

SOCKBRIDGE

Pooley
Bridge

ASKHAM

N

Dockray

Ullswater

Glenridding

Miles

DAY 4
Glenridding to Eamont Bridge

SUMMARY

Distance: 18.5 miles to village centre, or 20 miles to Lowther Park campsite (missing out Penrith).

Total Ascent: 2,559 feet (780 metres).

Expected Duration: 10 hours.

Map: 1:25000 Outdoor Leisure Series sheet No.5.

Terrain and Difficulty: Begins by climbing through steep hill country, but later takes in woods as well as undulating farmland and riverside scenery.

Highlights: Charming village architecture, a castle, a dramatic waterfall and splendid lake views.

Option: Penrith town centre and Wordsworth sites.

CAMPSITE OR BUNKBARN START

Leave the campsite at the toilet block end, crossing the bridge and turning left in front of the entrance to the bunkbarn. Walk up the track (signposted Greenside, Helvellyn via Myers Beck). Almost opposite the entrance to Gillside Farm take the track branching off on the right, and about 80 yards later reaching a gate. Ignore this and instead pass through a kissing gate over to its right.

From here follow a track contouring for approximately half a mile to join an old mining track (now used as a bridleway known as the Greenside Road) shortly after climbing up from a crossing over Glenridding Beck. Raise is the upsweeping mass forming the distant skyline, beyond the head of the valley, while the scree-streaked slope ascending to your right is the fine peak of Sheffield Pike.

When the bridleway is met turn left and follow this for about half a mile into Greenside, passing the youth hostel situated on the left upon entering the hamlet. This little nest of cottages is constructed in a style pleasing to the eye, utilising the native slate to good effect, yet marred by the tiers upon tiers of mining tips all around, above and beyond the settlement, forming a historic veneer that jars the senses.

Continue up the track passing a couple of iron horse troughs set in the roadside a few yards above the youth hostel. These rusting artefacts remind us of days before the advent of the motor car, when draught animals hauled equipment up the hill and returned with the ore. After crossing Swart Beck pass the Greenside Bury Jubilee Outdoor Pursuits Centre and, just beyond this, turn to the right (signposted Sticks Pass) to reach the Swirrel Bothy.

At the next bend beyond the bothy a three-way junction provides the path coming from straight ahead representing the alternative way from Red Tarn into Greenside the previous day. This path can be seen snaking its way down the side of Catstye Cam. Our continuing route from this junction, however, lies to the right, winding uphill (signposted to Brown Cove, Whiteside and Sticks Pass). This provides superb views, spoil heaps excluded, back down Glenridding towards Ullswater, backed by Place Fell with the High Street range beyond that.

Another parting of the ways is shortly met. Following the bridleway to the left would lead to Whiteside, but our way is to the right, well cairned, picking its way up through thickets of juniper bushes beneath the beetling crags of Stang End. The climb is certainly the steepest of the day, and in warm weather will certainly produce a head of steam. This hard-earned height alas will all too soon be lost again – an unfortunate fact, but one compensated for by the superb views and those to follow. The head of Glenridding is also good raptor country, so keep an eye open for buzzard and peregrine.

When the way more or less draws level with the top of the largest spoil heap, traces of what appear to be a derelict wall lead off up the screes to the left. This in fact is the collapsed remains of a flue which extended up the fellside to a chimney. Climbing further to where the path levels out, the old flue can be made out running for almost a mile up the Stang, the grassy eastern spur of Raise.

Ahead loom the remains of a dam once holding water for the mining operation. Just before reaching this, a less obvious path sneaks off to the right. Ignore this in favour of a route crossing a small footbridge and running alongside and eventually cutting through the north-eastern end of the dam embankment. The way is vague but guided across a chaotic

The spectacular Aira Force is a highlight of the stage between Glenridding and Eamont Bridge

area by a few well-spaced cairns. Up the valley can just be seen the 'A' frame structure of the Lake District Ski Club hut high on the slopes of Raise.

The bridleway soon swings north-north-west towards a disused quarry piercing the hillside ahead like a large, sightless eye socket. At the base of this, the Sticks Pass route turns left and our path, not obvious until some height is gained, turns off (point marked by a cairn) up the hillside immediately beneath the quarry. The way lies straight up the hill until just beyond the quarry a well-defined pathway contours around the hillside to reach the col at Nick Head. >>

The Sticks Pass route, the second-highest in Lakeland, has in times past been an important thoroughfare linking Patterdale with St Johns in the Vale and Wythburn. Greenside, however, owes its very existence to the local mining industry, its lead mine in particular having provided prosperity for at least three hundred years. Indeed it is believed that the Romans may have been the first to extract lead in this valley.

Today the valley head is still scarred by unsightly tailings and worried by remnants of its recent industrial heritage. The flue on the Stang originally provided the updraught for the lead smelting operation at Greenside and also doubled as a condenser in which particular lead ore in suspension could be recovered. Amazingly, the mines in the vicinity were the scene of some of the earliest underground testing of explosives. The aim of this was to determine the likely effects of detonating nuclear explosions below ground. Thankfully they declined to test these at Greenside.

>> From Nick Head a mountain trail takes a dramatic contouring line around Deepdale Slack, beneath the crags of Glencoyne Head and Scot Crag, to reach a point on a shoulder above Bell Knott that continentals would call a *belvedere*, or viewpoint, offering a grand panorama overlooking the length of Ullswater. This is a sight that brings to mind those picturesque lakes in north-western Italy, Como and Garda, a comparison that is by no means unfavourable.

After rounding the shoulder a faint path cairned off to the left is ignored and we continue forward across an area of boggy ground parallel to (but about 30 yards away from) a dry-stone wall. The path and wall soon converge, the latter remaining a companion for at least the next mile along the flank of Watermillock Common. This part of the walk is all the more pleasurable for the lack of climbing, allowing the walker to savour the unfolding vista. Where the wall takes off downhill, our way, still contouring, heads forward as the first buildings of Dockray hamlet come into sight.

The path descends across rough pastureland, with the mountain massif of Blencathra visible away in the distance to the north-west. At the outskirts of Dockray veer to the right along a farm track following this around a barn to reach a gate. Beyond this turn left up the road, go over the bridge and take the first track on the right, a footpath signposted to Aira Force and Ulcat Row (yellow waymark arrow). After about 120 yards ignore the turning right, over a cattle grid, and the footpath left for Ulcat Row. Instead go straight forward along a continuing track.

Pass through a gate and walk downhill towards Aira Beck before veering left between a house and a barn with an interesting weather vane. Shortly beyond the house, cross a footbridge and swing to the right meeting another path from the left. Continue beside a fence and through a gate in a wall, ignoring the permissive path heading left for Gowbarrow Fell. Not far ahead the well-made path enters a wood with High Force waterfall audible not far ahead.

Soon several paths lead to the right giving access to a footbridge and viewing platform overlooking a section of impressive narrow canyon. By keeping to the path nearest the true left banking, a single-arched bridge is eventually met spanning the gorge to give a wonderful bird's-eye view of Aira Force thundering into a plunge pool. A lower bridge is connected with the upper structure by a short, circular loop path up and down both sides of the ravine. In the summer months when the high sun allows its rays to penetrate the ravine, the spray generated by the cataract creates wonderful rainbows. >>

The fine waterfall of Aira Force provided a scene in two of Wordsworth's poems, *The Somnambulist* and *Aira Force Valley*. The woods embrace many arboreal species, including sweet chestnut and the Caledonian pine, and rare as it now unfortunately is this woodland haven remains home to the native red squirrel. On days when the woods are not crowded with visitors, walkers who are quiet may with luck spot one of these delightful creatures.

>> The continuing walk from Aira Force keeps to the uppermost path along the true left rim of the ravine, tracing the edge of the woods soon to reach a gate with the path

continuing straight forward. Turn left through the gate and walk forward and slightly left along a well-defined path to meet another junction after 150 yards. The way straight ahead goes down to the shore side Gallowbarrow Woods, famous in spring for Wordsworth's never-ending line of daffodils, and from where a devious footpath climbs steeply again to reach the airy viewpoint at Yew Crag.

At the time of writing the latter path was closed and not recommended due to the dangers of rockfall. The alternative is to take the rising line up the hillside from the junction previously mentioned, angling up beneath Hind Crag and giving views down towards Lyulph's Tower. Eventually the trail reaches a cairn at the Yew Crag viewpoint, an excellent spot for contemplating Wordsworth and one of his beloved lakes. Immediately across Ullswater can be seen Sandwick Bay and the entrance to Martindale, countryside that will beckon in two days' time. >>

Sandwick Bay is where Dorothy and William left their boat for a walking tour up Martindale with their friend Charles Luff. Lyulph's Tower was once the Duke of Norfolk's hunting lodge, the castellated structure erected on the site of an earlier building which, according to oral tradition, was itself erected on land owned by a Saxon chieftain, and after whom the present building is named.

Gowbarrow Park and its early-spring daffodils (*Narcissus pseudonarcissus*) gave rise to probably the most famous and widely quoted work of Wordsworth, the poem *Daffodils*. Dorothy recorded the fact of her and William finding the lakeside daffodils in her journal entry for April 1802:

> When we were in the woods beyond Gowbarrow Park we saw a few daffodils close to the water-side. We fancied that the lake had floated the seeds ashore, and that the little colony had sprung up. But as we went along there were more and yet more; and at last, under the boughs of the trees, we saw that there was a long belt of them along the shore.

>> From Yew Crag the path continues to rise slightly; contouring around to the left, it takes an obvious line between Great Meldrum and Swinburn's Park, easy walking through typical buzzard country. About three-quarters of a mile from the earlier viewpoint a stile is crossed in a wall by a ruined

barn, beyond which a conifer forest is entered. Since the original surveys were made, the small broadleaf wood marked on the map has now been overgrown by an extensive conifer forest.

The gently switchbacking trail is easy going and unambiguous but don't expect to see or hear much wildlife, for apart from a few tits and finches or the occasional buzzard quartering the clearings for rodents, these pine woods are pretty much devoid of living creatures. As far as forests go, this one is not unpleasant, however. Because it grows on a hillside it seems more open and there are frequent views over Ullswater and beyond, to the distant strip of indigo that is the Cross Fell range of the northern Pennines.

After leaving the forest behind continue along a fence to a wall corner, cross the stile here and proceed beside the wall to a kissing gate at the next corner. Beyond this cross a brook and then bear right on a descending path through bracken and gorse. After maybe quarter of a mile the way converges on and traces a wall and the continuing fence line, passing a vicarage and heading slightly uphill to meet a road.

Turn left along this road, pass the Cove Campsite and turn right at the first junction (signposted Bennet Head and Dacre). Proceed down the lane passing the Quiet Campsite on the left, and in about 50 yards pick up a footpath off to the left (fingerpost). Cross a stile and make for the far side of the pasture. Cross another stile here and, maintaining the same bearing, walk across the next field to yet a third stile at a wall end, and from there go straight to a ladder stile.

Keeping now to the fence line on your left, walk in the direction of Tongue, visible over the rise, but just before this pass through a gate, walk down the track and in a few yards cross a second farm track at right-angles. Walk a few paces forward with a fence on your left to a corner where the fence swings left, then continue forward along the same line to find a stile at the far side of the pasture. Beyond this veer slightly right to negotiate a further stile.

Cross the next fields towards Land Ends, go up a banking and continue through a small copse beside the cottage, tracing a route indicated by frequent marker posts. The way soon passes though more open, scrubby terrain, shortly reaching a gate beneath some power lines. Beyond the gate the path traverses pastureland once again.

Go straight forward from the power lines to a stile over a fence just before a field barn, passing the latter on its right-hand side and continuing straight forward for Grove Foot Farm, keeping close to the left side of the pasture. Soon the path turns left over a stile, then sharp right to continue now with farm buildings on your right. Proceed forward, recrossing the fence a few yards ahead, then walking in front of the house, through the farmyard and out the far side.

One of the strange stone 'bears' found in the Dacre village churchyard

Go through a gate and turn sharp left, skirting the perimeter of the field around the far left corner. About 50 yards from there a stile is reached. Cross it and take a direct line for the bottom right corner of the next field, passing close to a curious, multi-trunked spreading oak tree to enter the hamlet of Sparket at the road in front of Lanehead House. Continue across the road and down a track beside the house (public footpath).

Follow the way around a barn to the right, then turn left through the second gate, here marked with a white direction arrow. Walk forward between hedges, tracing the route slightly to the right alongside a denuded hedgerow, to the far right corner of the pasture. Pass through yet another gate. Turn left here, then right, walking beside the house and forward to find a stile in the right-hand fence corner just to one side of overhead power lines. Walk forward for about 30 yards following the power lines, then turn right along a footpath (a bearing of 60 degrees), not visible on the ground, but indicated by a line of posts bearing yellow arrows.

When a road is eventually reached turn left and proceed along it by Sparket Mill across Dacre Beck and on up the hill to Hutton John, close to the northern limits of the National Park boundary. Here the road climbs beside a small wood, but where this ends a footpath crosses the road. Turn right at this point and head down towards a ladder stile to the left of a barn, the Hutton John manor-house clearly visible over to the right.

From this hamlet an obvious right of way is traced across pastureland for approximately one mile, passing along the top side of a small wood at Brockhole Hag, to a point where Dacrebank Farm lies just ahead. Here the right of way proceeds alongside a wall until a stile allows this to be crossed (yellow arrows on posts). Walk straight forward up the field in the direction of a barn just visible over the rise, then bear left to cross a ladder stile. The village of Dacre can now be seen in the near distance.

From the stile strike across a large pasture making a beeline for the northernmost (left) visible point of the village, crossing the line of an old field boundary to where a gap stile allows entry to the road. Turn right into Dacre passing the turn-off for the church. Take the next left, a footpath signposted to Stainton, passing through a gate and turning sharp left, following a path around the perimeter of the church with the keep of Dacre Castle over to the right. >>

Dacre is a neat village, centred upon its interesting little church which is believed to have been built on the site of an Anglo-Saxon monastery mentioned by Bede in his Ecclesiastical History. The present building is entirely Norman, but inside can be seen fragments of carved masonry believed to date from the ninth century. Within the churchyard stand four curious carved stone bears, perhaps coming from the nearby castle. It was in Dacre in May 1804 that Dorothy Wordsworth met her sister-in-law's brother and sister, Tom and Sarah, after they had been worshipping.

The remains of Dacre Castle include a fortified pele tower which is contemporary with the time of the border raids between England and Scotland. This is a 14th-century structure modified by restorations in the 16th and 17th centuries. The castle was the focus of an unsuccessful rebellion in 1569 led by Leonard Dacre against Queen Elizabeth I.

>> From the next gate by the far corner of the churchyard continue up over the hill, keeping to the wall side to find a ladder stile in the far right corner of the field. Once over this negotiate the next rise and continue across pastureland along an obvious right of way negotiating further field boundaries by way of stiles. The route skirts around a small copse at length reaching two gates. Cross the stile adjacent to the left-hand side of the two and, keeping to a wall side, walk in the direction of Park House Farm. >>

Mary Wordsworth's brother, Tom Hutchinson, lived at Park House from 1804 till 1808, with his sisters Sarah and Joanna. Only half a mile away is Dalemain House, a Georgian-fronted building that is part medieval and part Tudor and which was once the ancestral seat of the Hasell family. It is now open to the public, the displays including a Chinese room and many fine paintings and pieces of furniture. The main claim to fame of Stainton village is that it supplied a serviceman who was a pall-bearer at the funeral of King Edward VIII in 1952.

>> The way skirts the farm along its left side to follow a wall uphill slightly to reach a gate. Go through this and turn right, afterwards proceeding forward and across a ladder stile by the edge of a small conifer wood. Beyond this trace a fence line along the right-hand side of the field to pass through

either of two gates by a line of trees. At this point yellow arrows indicate footpaths to the left and right. Our way follows neither, but aims (path not visible on the ground) across the next field towards the top left corner. Here the path crosses a stile and for a few paces runs parallel with the linear wood.

When a gate is reached enter the trees but shortly vacate them again at a ladder stile into a narrow pasture. An isolated outcrop of limestone leads around a corner to the left where a gate gives onto a pleasant green lane from which Penrith town can be glimpsed away to the east. After half a mile the lane enters Stainton, the road being followed down through the village and straight forward when the crossroads is met.

A few yards beyond the village green turn right by a house called Mains and some 60 yards along here turn left through a gate and a stile. Continue along the wall edge to pick up and cross a stile in the far right corner. Go half right over a stream gully and towards a wall corner. Maintaining the same bearing up a banking, pass through a stile in a wall, then bear half left to the far corner of the field to enter the road.

Turn right out of Stainton along the unclassified road passing Megbank, but after only 60 yards turn down a walled lane and its continuation across the A592 Pooley Bridge Road to reach the River Eamont at Stainton Island. Take the path off to the left (signposted Yanwath and Tirril) a few yards before the Eamont and trace an obvious path keeping to the riverbank through fields and woods as far as the footbridge half a mile distant.

Cross to the far bank and turn left. A few yards in front a right of way strikes off half right, uphill across a cultivated area directly for Sockbridge, but the continuation for Eamont Bridge is left (signposted Yanwath) along the wooded true right bank of the river. Very soon the trees are left behind at a stile. After crossing a footbridge go straight forward along the riverside. At the far side of the meadow trace the path around to the right for a few yards then head left over a stile.

Walk up the banking and follow the edge of the wooded riverbank. Cross another stile beneath overhead power lines to a second stile. Beyond this the hedgerow on your left is followed into the far corner, where yet another stile allows a crossing into the next field. Turn right here and, with the hedge now on your right, and Yanwath Hall visible away to your left, walk as far as the corner and turn left through a gate into the lane.

Turn right beneath the railway, then left through the gate and forward a few yards. Turn right immediately after a cottage known as The Mews. Continue forward between two fences, the property over to the left being The Grotto, once the home of Wordsworth's friend, Thomas Wilkinson. Pass through a gate and walk forward along a fence side beneath a line of mature elm trees, following these around a right corner to where the pasture pinches in and briefly becomes a green lane before opening out again into the neighbouring paddock. >>

Yanwath is a small village two miles south of Penrith. It is unfortunately sited between the mainline railway and the busy M6 motorway. Yanwath Hall is today a farmhouse and part of the Lowther estate, incorporating a very fine 13th-century pele tower. Thomas Wilkinson, a Quaker, was born at Yanwath. He was a keen gardener and Master of the Grounds for the Lowther estates. He was the owner of the spade honoured in William's verse, *The Spade of a Friend*. The Grotto is situated a little to the south-east of Yanwath Hall and it was to Wilkinson that William turned in 1806 to act as go-between in negotiations for a property he was interested in buying at Broad How in Patterdale.

>> Follow the left-hand fence around to a kissing gate, then proceed straight forward passing a ladder stile on the left, to continue into the far corner adjacent to the M6 motorway. Turn left through a stile here and walk parallel to the motorway between fences until you can walk beneath the carriageway and right up a metalled road for about 80 yards. At this point pick up a footpath on the left for Eamont Bridge.

Proceed alongside the house and, keeping to the left side of the field, eventually pick up a stile leading into the access road to Bleach Green. While crossing this field note the ramparts of the prehistoric Mayburgh Henge in the neighbouring field to the right. Turn right and follow the Bleach Green road beside the river into the village of Eamont Bridge.

Those wishing to visit Penrith town centre (30 minutes' walk) for supplies, overnight accommodation or perhaps to visit sites connected with William Wordsworth, should from this point follow directions as for Penrith Town Centre Option, as below. Otherwise, to reach the campsite turn south (right) along the A6 through the village. Walk out of Eamont

Yanwath Hall and its fine pele tower, seen on Day 4 between Stainton and Eamont Bridge

Bridge passing the junction with the B5320 where King Arthur's Round Table can be seen in the adjacent field. A short distance down the road from this Neolithic henge monument turn right down the mile-long driveway into the Lowther Park caravan and camping site which forms a part of the extensive Lowther estate. >>

Mayburgh Henge consists of a banking formed from river cobbles and, like its smaller neighbour, probably dates from the Neolithic or New Stone Age around 1800BC. It has a single standing stone near its centre. Brougham Hall, located east of the A6 just to the south of the river crossing at Eamont Bridge, is an elegant residence once rented by Captain John Wordsworth, the poet's cousin, after he had retired from a career at sea. William stayed here with his wife in 1805.

The 18th-century Beehive Inn at Eamont Bridge was once kept by a Jacobite chaplain-turned-innkeeper following the failure of the 1745 Rebellion. The Scottish army accompanying Prince Charles south to Worcester is said to have camped within the banking of King Arthur's Round Table monument.

Lowther Castle (not visible from the campsite or the continuing route to Askham) was built in the early years of the

19th century, replacing an earlier structure which stood on the site of Lowther Hall. Mary Queen of Scots spent a night here before her imprisonment in Carlisle Castle. A fire in the 1950s left only a shell as a reminder of the castle's former glory. The Lowthers were originally granted land in the Lake District by Edward I in 1283 and went on to become one of the most influential families in the north.

For four generations the Lowthers provided the principal income of the Wordsworths. William's father, John, was land agent to Sir James Lowther (1736–1802), first Earl of Lonsdale. Other members of the Lowther family are famous for the Lonsdale Belts of boxing, and for the connections with the Automobile Association, the fifth Earl being its first president.

PENRITH TOWN CENTRE OPTION

Cross the road, go through a gate and turn left over the footbridge to walk up the road in the direction of Penrith. Cross to the opposite side of the road and just before the A66 pass through a gate on the left. Follow a footpath veering around to the right, behind a cottage, through a stile and across a small field thick with yellow ragwort to reach a kissing gate a few yards ahead.

Cross the A66 by the roundabout and continue as if heading for Penrith. Instead, however, pick up a footpath leading off left (signposted to Weatheriggs Lane). The metalled path passes between a hedge and fence and leads to a residential estate. Weatheriggs Lane continues past the school and Penrith Cricket Club to become Castle Hill Road, soon reaching a turn-off to a recycling centre and carpark.

Just beyond this, follow the road around to the right to enter the town centre at a large open area. At the far side of this, walk down the narrow Angel Lane into Market Square. At the Middlegate end of Market Square will be found a draper's and millinery shop. A plaque on the wall announces that this was once the home of the Cooksons, William's grandparents. William often spent time here until, in 1799, the nine-year-old was packed off to school in Hawkshead.

A right turn out of Market Place leads to King Street where, a few yards down on the right will be found the Robin Hood Inn, where William's friend, Raisley Calvert, once stayed.

Being close to the border country, Penrith has occupied a strategic position, a crossroads in history, since time immemorial, and has suffered as a consequence. The Romans passed this way along their ambitious road over High Street and built their fort (Voreda) a few miles to the north. In 1314 the town was razed by the Scots after the Battle of Bannockburn and fired again 31 years later. The castle was erected in the 14th century simply as a fortified tower; it was later added to by Richard, Duke of Gloucester, the future King Richard III. It now lies in ruins just to the east of the railway station.

Ecclesiastical buildings suffered a similar fate, the surviving St Andrew's Church having a Norman tower; the interior is pretty much as the young William and Dorothy would have remembered it from the time when they lodged with their guardians, the Cooksons. Outside the church is a mound topped by two Anglo-Scandinavian crosses which for some reason are referred to as the Giant's Grave. Near by, a curious red sandstone building, part of a restaurant, is thought to have been Dame Birkett's school where William, Dorothy and Mary Hutchinson, William's future love, received tuition. In Portland Place another wall plaque indicates that a building now housing the library was once another Wordsworth residence, that of the poet's cousin, John.

The wooded hill rising behind the town is Penrith Beacon, and a short climb leads easily to the monument at its summit. The Beacon was once a link in the nation's early-warning communication chain. It overlooks the town on its north side, and it is where the six-year-old William, out riding with a family servant, became separated from his companion and came upon the place where a murderer had been gibbeted. He was suitably terrified and in later years referred to the experience, and the associated sight of a young girl carrying a pitcher of water, as being one of the visionary 'spots in time' often experienced by the poet. The view from the top of the Beacon, especially at sunset, is wonderful.

USEFUL INFORMATION

Accommodation: Choice of guest-houses, hotels and B&Bs in Penrith. B&B in Eamont Bridge.

Bunkhouse: None.

Camping: Lowther Park Caravan and Campsite, Eamont Bridge. Full facilities, bar and supermarket. £3/night/person. Open 17 March to 9 November, inclusive. Tel: (01768) 863631.

Youth Hostel: None.

Transport: Service No.108 links Penrith with Patterdale serving Yanwath Cottages, Pooley Bridge, Gowbarrow Cottages, Park Brow Foot and Glenridding.

Supplies: Good choice of stores in Penrith. Shop at the Quiet Site (camping), Watermillock.

Refreshments: Pubs in Dacre and Eamont Bridge. Several pubs and cafés in Penrith.

Tourist Information: Middlegate, Penrith. Tel: (017687) 72803.

DAY 5
Eamont Bridge to Pooley Bridge

SUMMARY
Distance: 9.5 miles.
Total Ascent: 236 feet (72 metres).
Expected Duration: 3 hours.
Map: 1:25000 Outdoor Leisure Series sheet No.5.
Terrain and Difficulty: A short stage with little climbing.
Highlights: Prehistoric sites, idyllic villages and interesting churches with Wordsworthian connections.
Option: None.

PENRITH TOWN CENTRE START
Walkers who have stayed overnight in the town centre should retrace the previous day's steps into Eamont Bridge, and from there go down the river through Yanwath to the footbridge just north of Sockbridge.

To continue south-west for Pooley Bridge turn sharp left (signposted Tirril and Sockbridge) immediately before the footbridge, just where the path emerges from its wooded riverside course. Walk uphill across agricultural land (taking care not to tread on growing crops) following a diagonal line towards the village of Sockbridge, seen up ahead. Aim for a huge oak tree and find and cross a stile just to its right.

Continue forward and slightly to the right to reach a double gap stile at a wall junction by some cottages. Cross the first wall and then go immediately left over the second stile, walking downhill across a small paddock to pass through a stile to the left of a cottage and here enter the road. At this point the main route, starting at the Lowther Park campsite, joins from the left. Turn right here through the village and go on as at Main Route Continuation.

LOWTHER PARK CAMPSITE START
To continue for Pooley Bridge, exit the campsite at its southernmost extremity and from the stile here follow the

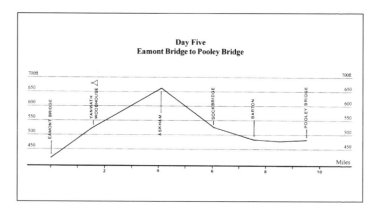

Day Five
Eamont Bridge to Pooley Bridge

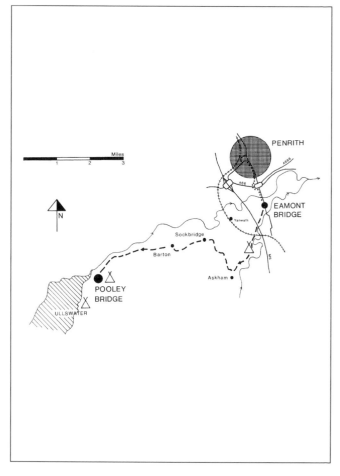

THE WILLIAM WORDSWORTH WAY

estate road without deviation through mature woodland until the river bridge is reached. Take off to the right here, through an iron gate and up a steep banking, to follow an unmarked trail through mixed woodland more or less parallel with the river for about quarter of a mile.

Soon the path skirts the top edge of the woods, between there and adjacent farmland, before briefly descending again. Not far ahead look for and turn along a footpath branching off to the right (marked by an arrow on a post). Within a few yards cross a ladder stile at a wall, and from here take a line half left diagonally across the pasture with the village of Askham over on your left, the castellated Askham Old Hall being obvious. Cross a stile here and turn right along a short bridleway to its junction with a metalled lane and turn right again. >>

Askham is a pretty village, its -*ham* place-name component betraying its Anglo-Saxon roots, and meaning a place where ash trees grow. It is situated across the river from the Lowther estate. William visited the Church of St Peter here when staying as a guest of the Lowthers at the nearby castle. The Elizabethan Askham Hall is the home of the present Earl of Lonsdale.

>> After passing Barnet Wood, take off left (fingerpost) along a green lane extending to a gate by a disused reservoir. Through this, go straight forward to a second gate; instead of passing through this, walk to the right alongside the wall to yet a third gate where the official right of way, as marked on the map, is straight forward. Crops have been planted here, however, and the way is diverted left through a gate and immediately right along a fence line. In the distance over in the west the massif of Blencathra looks a little like South Africa's Table Mountain.

At the corner turn right through the gate and left at a gap stile. Aim for the left-hand corner of a small wood, go through a stile and walk forward through a gate and down a lane leading towards Tirril. Continue down this lane to its junction with the B5320 Pooley Bridge Road and turn left. Immediately after the general store and post office turn right following the left side of the paddock, down a narrowing of the field leading into a leafy tunnel, and trace this to a road. Turn left here to meet the path representing the alternative start from Penrith centre a few paces ahead.

MAIN ROUTE CONTINUATION

Continue up the road through Sockbridge to the first T-junction. If you turn right here into the oldest part of the village, the second house on the left is known as Wordsworth House and is its most elegant residence. Continue forward, however, passing this junction and, when the road swings left, continue on a bridleway (signposted Thorpe) adjacent to Quakers Lane.

The way passes through this hamlet after a couple of hundred yards or so then continues for almost half a mile further to the B5320. Turn right here and shortly right again up a metalled lane (bridleway) to Barton St Michaels Church, an interesting structure with a curious centrally positioned tower. Continuing from the lychgate follow the lane around the east side of the church to Barton Church Farm. Where the right of way then turns right in front of a row of houses, pass through a farmyard.

From here turn left over a small stream. Go left again (fingerpost) over a ladder stile and from there trace the farm track forward to a gate. Walk left then right along the farm track to where the bridleway turns left (sign for Pooley Bridge). Walk in the direction of a barn but just before this turn right beside a fence to a gate, and beyond this right once more, following the perimeter of the fence to a parting of the ways. >>

Sockbridge has many connections with Wordsworth. William's paternal grandfather, Richard, lived here and the poet's father owned some land near by which he inherited from his brother, Richard, who lived at Sockbridge Hall (now named Wordsworth House). William often visited with his sister, Dorothy, and later with his wife, Mary.

Barton Church is transitional in style – that is, midway between Norman and Early English. It sits upon an ancient foundation in a circular churchyard which possibly has pagan origins. It has a curious central tower. In the Middle Ages people converged upon Barton from as far away as Kirkstone Pass, the old Roman road along High Street being the route used by worshippers.

William's grandparents, Richard and Mary, are interred here, and brass plaques commemorating them can be seen in the chancel. Richard led a distinguished life. He was born in Yorkshire in 1690 and was the first of the family to settle in

Barton Church, where the poet's grandfather is interred

Westmoreland. He subsequently became Clerk of the Peace, and at the time of the 1745 Rebellion was Receiver General for Westmoreland as well as Agent to the Lowther estates.

>> A right turn here will take you to Dacre, but we turn left for Pooley Bridge instead. Walk slightly uphill to pass through a gate. A few yards beyond, the route dives into a narrow, overgrown path between fences. (This can be somewhat nettly so be careful if you're wearing shorts!) Soon the way divides a second time, our route turning right through a kissing gate and left along a footpath. Cross a stile after a few steps, then trace the right-hand edge of the pasture with the rounded, forested hill of Dunmallet seen immediately in front.

Once over the rise pass through another gate and walk forward to a stile at the far side of the pasture, before heading for Hole House Farm. Upon entering this bear right down past Riverside Cottage, between a barn and houses and through a gate. Bear right down the banking and trace the obvious path upstream beside the river. In very severe weather these riverside pastures may flood.

Pooley Bridge is entered behind the Sun Inn. To reach the campsite at Hillcroft Park, turn left through the village and fork right (signposted Howtown and Martindale) by the tiny church, walking up the hill to a crossroads. Continue forward up Roe Head Lane to find the entrance to the campsite on the left after 200 yards.

Walkers may opt to stay overnight at the Waterside House campsite, a mile further down the lake shore, as an alternative to Hillcroft Park. To reach the site follow the first part of Day 6's route guide. Walkers should note that apart from small shops at the Waterside House, Side Farm and Sykeside campsites, there will be no further opportunity to buy supplies until Grasmere at the end of Day 7, assuming that the shops etc are not closed by the time you get there. It would perhaps be better to stock up here in Pooley Bridge for the next two days.

Pooley Bridge straddles the boundary between the old counties of Cumberland and Westmoreland and historically has little to distinguish it, though across the river the *-dun* place-name component of the wooded hill, Dunmallet, suggests a fortified site at some time in the past. Indeed, a prehistoric earthwork here has revealed, among other artefacts, a number of pre-Iron Age stone axe heads.

A little out of the village on the south side is Eusemere, the former home of Catherine Clarkson, an intimate friend of Dorothy and the wife of anti-slavery campaigner Thomas Clarkson. The Wordsworths often visited the Clarksons, travelling via either the Kirkstone Pass or by way of Grizedale and Patterdale. William's cousin John made Eusemere his family home after the Clarksons vacated it, and lived there until his death in 1819.

USEFUL INFORMATION

Accommodation: Hotels, guest-houses and B&Bs in Pooley Bridge.

Bunkhouse: None.

Camping: Hillcroft Park, Pooley Bridge. Full facilities. £4/night/person. Open summer only. Tel: (017684) 86363. Waterside House, Pooley Bridge. Full facilities. £4.50/night/person. Open summer. Tel: (017684) 86332.

Youth Hostel: None.

Transport: Service No.108 linking Penrith with Patterdale serves Yanwath Cottages and Pooley Bridge.

Supplies: Shop and post office in Tirril. Shops and post office in Pooley Bridge. Camping Gaz and Coleman/Epigas cartridges available.

Refreshments: Pub in Tirril. Inns and cafés in Pooley Bridge.

Tourist Information: The Square, Pooley Bridge. Tel: (017684) 86530.

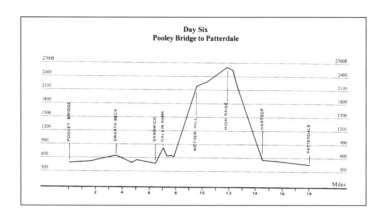

Day Six
Pooley Bridge to Patterdale

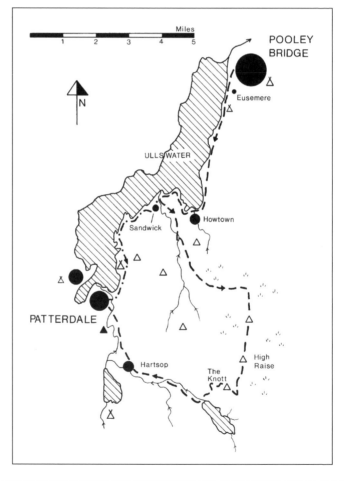

DAY 6
Pooley Bridge to Patterdale

SUMMARY

Distance: 18 miles (to YHA hostel). Add 0.75 mile to campsite. If low-level option is taken, it's only 11 miles.

Total Ascent: 2,795 feet (852 metres).

Expected Duration: 6–7 hours (4 hours for low-level option).

Map: 1:25000 Outdoor Leisure Series sheet No.5.

Terrain and Difficulty: Easy lakeside paths are contrasted with high ridge sections, in places tracing the Roman road, High Street.

Highlights: Superb lake scenery (low-level option). Dramatic mountain scenery (high-level normal route).

Option: Low-level lakeside route avoiding mountains in bad weather.

The lakeside path between Pooley Bridge and Patterdale is the route most likely to have been taken by the young William when returning to Penrith during holidays from school in Hawkshead. A mixture of footpaths and short stretches of quiet road extend between Pooley Bridge and Patterdale via Howtown and Sandwick Bay, beyond which a pleasant bridle-way links with Patterdale as a low-level switchback option to Martindale Common and High Street. The lower-level route may be chosen or preferred when bad weather necessitates avoiding the high ground.

From the Sun Inn in Pooley Bridge walk south-west to where the main road leaps across the river bridge and here carry straight on along the driveway for Eusemere (public footpath). Only a few yards ahead the way splits, our footpath taking off to the right between a house and a garage. From this point a pleasant lakeshore path is traced for one mile, the route well marked and easy to follow. A short distance along this path is a good view of Eusemere over to the left. At length the shore path enters Waterside House campsite, through which the right of way extends.

Rejoin the road at the southern extremity of the campsite and turn right. Proceed along the road for quarter of a mile, ignoring the first footpath taking off on the left and instead taking the next track (fingerpost) heading up to Cross Dormont Farm. Bear right over a stile (fingerpost) just before the house and walk around the rear of a barn, over a second stile, and from here cross the pasture for Seat Farm.

Passing this on its right side walk around to the left behind it, keeping to the left side of the pasture to cross a stile and then turn right. With a wall now on your right continue forward, tantalised by the magnificent mountain views extending to far-off Helvellyn, a scene evoking memories of the walk three days earlier. At the far side of the field go through a gate, pass Crook-a-dyke Farm on its right-hand side and go down a track signposted for Howtown and Martindale.

After about 60 yards veer left through a gate then sharp right along a wall to avoid Thwaite Farm. From the gate beyond this, walk along a wall side to a corner and from there, keeping the same bearing, cross a rough pasture dotted with gorse to intersect a wall which is followed forward to a gate. This gives access to a fenced-off enclosure, through which, still keeping to the wall, a gate is met in its far left corner.

Turn left on a track leading uphill to Auterstone Farm, passing the house on its left and turning along a track leading left and uphill to join an obvious bridleway. Turn right here and follow the trail into Howtown Wyke. This provides a slightly more elevated route than the footpaths nearer the lake, and the superb lake and mountain views are a bonus. On the left the craggy slopes of Barton Fell and Arthur's Pike overshadow the route.

The way is clear and unambiguous for the next mile and a half, providing easy walking with no route-finding difficulties, so why not do as I did and switch on to auto-pilot and simply enjoy the scenery.

When the bridleway draws alongside the first building on the outskirts of Howtown, a house incorporating round chimney stacks (more about these later), our way leaves the bridleway on a footpath leading right, down a banking to a gate. Turn left through this, walk past a static caravan and through a second gate. From here aim for the bottom-left corner of the pasture where a third gate leads into the road.

Cross the latter and go through a gate to follow a lakeside path for Sandwick and Patterdale. This passes Howtown pier and shortly intersects a track, which is followed forward towards Waternook. About 30 yards ahead bear left through a gate and uphill through the trees to meet another path at right-angles. Turn to the right, behind the house, and trace a pleasant terrace walk with views down Ullswater towards Dunmallet. After the Geordie Crag viewpoint the way dives into the predominantly oak cover of Hallinhag Wood, before finally turning into Sandwick Bay. >>

Where the lakeside path skirts around Howton Wyke, across on the far shore can be seen an outward bound centre and the Old Church Hotel. These were formerly known as Halsteads and Old Church respectively, and both were once owned by John Marshall and his son James, who were friends of the Wordsworths. John had wed a friend of Dorothy, who herself was also a very good friend of the Marshall sisters. Sandwick Bay is where William and Dorothy Wordsworth disembarked from their boat and, with their friend, Charles Luff, began a walking tour up Martindale.

>> After leaving the trees follow a broad pathway across pastureland, soon entering Sandwick over a footbridge. Turn left here and walk up the road a few yards to where cars are usually parked. At this point the walker must make a decision, based upon personal fitness, available daylight and prevailing weather, on whether to follow the continuing lakeside path into Patterdale, or to take the longer and harder route via Martindale and the High Street range. If choosing the latter, follow the route directions for High Street Continuation, as below.

LAKESIDE LOW-LEVEL OPTION
Leave Sandwick Bay at the carpark terminating the metalled road by picking up a bridleway by Town Head cottage, a stony track heading uphill beside a wall to the south-west. After three-quarters of a mile the path crosses a beck after which Scalehow Force (waterfall) may be seen cascading over some slabs up to the left. The bridleway then climbs steeply beside the wall for about 35 yards, turns a corner and descends towards the lake.

Around the first headland beyond Scalehow Wood can be seen Lyulph's Tower (see Day 4) on the far shore of the lake.

Ullswater seen from the shore path just south of Pooley Bridge

The route at this point along the lakeside bridleway presents a pleasant switchback trail ducking through birch woodland and offering superb views of Ullswater, especially from the Devil's Chimney and Silver Point.

As you approach the promontory known as the Devil's Chimney, Stybarrow Crag can be seen across the lake, backed by a rising rocky spur terminating at Sheffield Pike. Not far beyond Purse Point the obvious trail passes Blowick House, seen through the trees over the wall on your right. Just by a barn a quarter of a mile later, the bridleway slips past the entrance to Blowick, and a little further, also on the right, is the campsite. To stay the night here walkers must book at Side Farm, almost half a mile's walk beyond the site. >>

The two promontories of Purse Point and the Devil's Chimney are significant in the long-running debate among scholars of Wordsworth. Either of these points could, so it is claimed, have been where William stole from the shore of Ullswater in a boat taken without the consent of the owner, while on his way 'home' to his grandparents in Penrith from school at Hawkshead. It was a moonlit night and the subsequent event, well documented in his autobiographical poem *The Prelude* (i.372–427), graphically illustrates the fright he experienced when overshadowed by a 'huge mountain black and huge'. The only detail omitted was the precise location of this event.

>> To reach the youth hostel, hotels or B&Bs in Patterdale, or to continue the William Wordsworth Way after camping, pass straight through Side Farm and beyond Side Cottage to reach a gate. Go through this and stroll forward down the metalled lane with Greenrigg House on the right. Here the road bends around to the right at a T-junction where it meets the main route, a lane from the left, coming from Hartsop after the long descent from High Street.

The cottage on the right after rounding the bend is today known as Wordsworth's Cottage and stands on land called Broad How, once owned by the poet. Continue down the lane to Goldrill Bridge. Walkers wishing to stay at the YHA hostel should cross the river and turn left up the road. The hostel is on the left just a few minutes' walk up the road. To reach the hotels and guest-houses in Patterdale turn right after crossing the bridge.

Tarn Beck in the Duddon Valley featured in one of Wordsworth's
famous sonnets about this area (Day 11)

Dora's Field, known as The Rash in Wordsworth's day, is carpeted with wild daffodils in early spring (Day 7)

Stone Arthur is glimpsed through autumn tree cover on
Butterlip Howe, Grasmere (Day 7/8)

ABOVE: A stormy day accentuates the boisterous Easedale Beck (Day 8)

BELOW: Bluebells and birch woodlands in the Duddon Valley

Langdale and the Furness Fells seen from the Langdale Pikes optional ascent (Day 8)

ABOVE: Woodlands near a spot named John's Grove by the Wordsworth household, in memory of William's brother (Day 7)

BELOW: On Day 10 the William Wordsworth Way passes through Eskdale. Harter Fell can be seen on the left of the picture

ABOVE: The Langdale Pikes reflected in a placid Blea Tarn; scenes from Wordsworth's *The Excursion* (Day 8)

BELOW: Walkers closely follow in Wordsworth's footsteps as they pass through Grizedale between Patterdale and Grasmere (Day 7)

Wastwater and a patchwork of enclosures at Wasdale Head. The route passes through this dramatic valley head on Day 12

HIGH STREET CONTINUATION

From Sandwick carpark continue for quarter of a mile up the quiet road then turn left over a bridge. Follow a lane through a gate (signposted Swinsty) and before long this leads to a gate by another farm. Turn left up a narrow grassy path climbing between walls at length to rejoin the road. Turn left along this for only ten yards then head right along a track taking off at a tangent, a bridleway giving views up Martindale and traced for half a mile to Winter Crag.

Turn left here and follow the road over the bridge and on to the tiny Church of St Martin, an interesting building mentioned by Wordsworth in his walking tour here in 1805. The continuing path takes off to the south-east immediately behind the church. Here an obvious path takes a slightly rising line beneath Steel Knotts for quarter of a mile. When more or less level with a field barn, look for a footpath marked on the Ordnance Survey map, which at this point assumes a vague line of green up through the bracken-covered slopes. >>

It is claimed that the Church of St Martin marks the site of 750 years of continuous Christian worship. The larger of the

Martindale. The route takes to the skyline forming the left flank of the valley

two yew trees in the churchyard was also mentioned by the poet and is reputed to be 1,300 years old. The church is said to be the parish chapel 'girt round with bare ring of mossy wall' as mentioned in his poem *The Brothers*.

>> The way is more a shallow gully than a path, but after climbing about 400 feet this then meets another, more obvious path coming from the left. Turn right and walk along this, passing through a ruined wall just above the wood at Nettle-howe Crag and continue to climb, more steeply now, with excellent views up the valley. The rounded spur of The Nab can be seen dividing the dale into two, the right-hand (western) branch being Bannerdale.

As the route ascends towards Gowk Hill the last dwelling in Martindale can be glimpsed at Dale Head, while the distant headwaters of Ramps Gill are cut off by the highest point of the day, High Raise (2,631 feet), Rampsgill Head and The Knott. Looking back, the views down Fusedale and Martindale to Ullswater, are no less dramatic. >>

Martindale is one of the few secluded corners of the Lake District that remain almost unchanged since the time Wordsworth took his walking tour in 1805. A graphic step-by-step account of this journey was included in his *Guide to the Lakes*, first published in 1810. The isolated valley forms a part of the Martindale Common within the ownership of the Dalemain House estate, and of which some 3,212 acres (1,300 hectares) has been declared a Site of Special Scientific Interest. The solitary dwelling of Dale Head is where William, Dorothy and Charles Luff were entertained during their excursion through the valley.

>> After rounding Brownthwaite Crag the way levels out briefly and even loses some hard-won height to contour around the headwaters of Fusedale. Pass through a gap in the wall and walk past two ruined field barns. Cross a stream and then bear right tracing the path, faint at first, then after re-crossing the stream continuing as a more obvious path. This takes a gradual line along the western flanks of Wether Hill, eventually crossing the head of Mere Beck before adopting a less gruelling approach to Red Crag following a fence line. This joins the main drag of High Street just before the summit.

Like countless thousands before us stretching back to the days of the Romans, and probably even earlier, we now follow the line of the old military highway along a broad, grassy ridge for a further mile and three-quarters, across the summit of High Raise at last, over Rampsgill Head noting Kidsty Pike away to the left, and down to a wall just before the broad col at the Straits of Riggindale. The scenery here can only be described as sumptuous, the ridge dropping precipitously away into Riggindale, leading to flooded Mardale, and rising ahead to the plateau of High Street itself. Away in the east can be seen the rounded range of the Howgills and to the west Fairfield and the mountains above Deepdale. >>

High Street is a range of mountains, and also their highest point, deriving its name from the fact that a Roman military road traversed the length of it, presumably linking the fort at Ambleside (Galava) with that at Brougham (Brocavum). It was almost certainly a route used by the ancient Britons before the arrival of the *Pax Romana*, and provided an obvious line of advance into the former county of Cumberland for the marauding Scots. It also served as a corpse road, worshippers travelling along here to the church at Barton (see Day 5) from Kirkstone Pass and Patterdale.

The plateau-like summit of High Street has seen competitive horseracing in the past, and along the flanks of this range fell ponies, perhaps direct descendants of real wild fell ponies, may with luck be seen upon these windswept heights. At the time I walked this stage of the route I was excited to come across three beautiful black ponies gambolling free along the upper reaches of Fusedale.

>> From the col a right turn gives easy walking along the broad path towards the rounded hill of The Knott, tracing the bridleway around its northern slopes before winding down towards the dam at Hayeswater. Don't make the mistake of following the footpath branching off (grid ref 43201295) to the right leading to Angle Tarn.

Cross the footbridge by the dam and bear right down the stony track until a bridge allows the route to cross over and continue down the true right side of the beck. Enter Hartsop after a further half-mile and walk down the lane to its junction with the A592 valley road. By continuing out of Hartsop along the main road for quarter of a mile, a site connected with Wordsworth is reached at Brothers Bridge, where Goldrill Beck flows out of Brothers Water. >>

It was at Brothers Bridge that William and Dorothy rested after crossing the Kirkstone Pass, perhaps on their way to visit the Luffs. Brothers Bridge and Brothers Water derive their names, so local tradition accords, from the fact that tragedies overtook two brothers from distinct local families, rather than from any connection with the poem *The Brothers*. The poem *Written in March* was composed here.

There is a campsite behind the Brotherswater Inn which can be reached (a 20-minute walk) by following a footpath from Brothers Bridge along the western side of the lake to Hartsop Hall and then east from there. It can also be reached by leaving Hartsop near the ford, and following a footpath south-west to the main road, where a permissive path leads the remainder of the way.

>> For the continuation to Grasmere tomorrow, however, it is more convenient to camp at Patterdale. To continue down the valley from Hartsop turn right along a bridleway, metalled at first, that leads off a few yards before the lane out of Hartsop joins the A592. When a junction is reached continue straight forward for Crook Beck; then, when the lane turns right for Hartsop Fold, walk along the continuing dirt track.

With the metalled surface left behind the way now becomes a pleasant bridleway passing Dubhow and a branch heading for Boardale Hause that steeply climbs up the hill to the right. Ignore this and another bridleway off to the left beyond the next gate. At Crook Beck Farm a path circumnavigates the buildings to rejoin the lane beyond. Turn right here and follow this past Rooking to where a metalled lane is met on a sweeping bend by Wordsworth House, a property once known as Broad How. At this point the low-level option from Sandwick Bay is joined coming from the right.

Those wishing to camp should turn right up the lane and follow this to Side Farm, a few minutes' walk away, where booking can be made for the campsite a quarter of a mile beyond. For alternative accommodation continue left down the lane from Wordsworth House as far as Goldrill Bridge. Those wishing to stay at the YHA hostel should cross the river and turn left up the road. The hostel is on the left just a few minutes up the road. For hotels and guest-houses in Patterdale turn right after crossing the bridge.

The Wordsworths often stayed at Side Farm, called Side in those days, when visiting Charles Luff and his wife. It was during the Martindale excursion that Charles pointed out to William the remains of a lowly chapel secreted at Boardale

Hause. This site was subsequently incorporated into a 'scene' in William's poem *The Excursion*, a description of which can be found in his *Guide to the Lakes*.

Broad How is a 19-acre property which Wordsworth owned between 1806 and 1834. He first saw it in the summer of 1806 during a visit to relations in Patterdale. At that time William and Dorothy came across the land for sale close to the head of Ullswater. Through their good friend Thomas Wilkinson of Yanwath (see Day 4), an offer of eight hundred pounds was made but not accepted. They subsequently forgot about the property until the Earl of Lonsdale intervened with financial assistance to help purchase the land. In the end, one thousand pounds was paid for the land, the Earl making up the difference. Though clearly grateful for this charitable act William was at the same time infuriated because he believed it an outrageous asking price.

USEFUL INFORMATION

Accommodation: Hotels and B&Bs in Patterdale.

Camping: Sykeside camping site, Brothers Water. Open all year with full facilities, including shop, bar and restaurant. £1.80/night/person plus £1.80/tent. Tel: (017684) 82239. Also at Side Farm, Patterdale. Open all year with full facilities, including small shop at farmhouse. £3.50/night/person. Tel: (017684) 82337.

Youth Hostel: Goldrill House, Patterdale. Tel: (017684) 82394.

Transport: Service No.108 links Penrith with Patterdale serving Pooley Bridge, Gowbarrow Cottages, Park Brow Foot and Glenridding.

Supplies: Shop at Sykeside campsite, Brothers Water.

Refreshments: Hotel with bar in Howtown. Hotel and cafés in Patterdale.

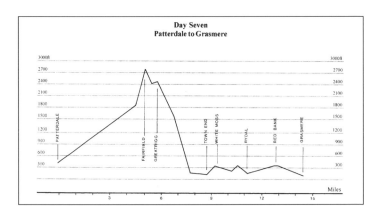

Day Seven
Patterdale to Grasmere

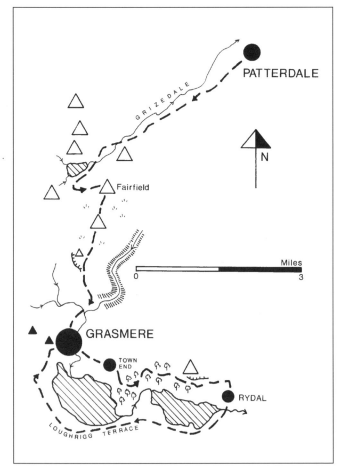

THE WILLIAM WORDSWORTH WAY

DAY 7
Patterdale to Grasmere

SUMMARY
Distance: 14.5 miles (to village centre and Butterlip How YHA hostel). Add a further 0.5 mile to Thorney How YHA hostel.

Total Ascent: 3,100 feet (945 metres).

Expected Duration: 6 hours.

Map: 1:25000 Outdoor Leisure Series sheet Nos.5, 7.

Terrain and Difficulty: This stage crosses the range of mountains west of Patterdale, the first half being a gradual stroll up Grizedale, followed by a tough climb to Fairfield summit. The day finishes with a leisurely stroll through woods and along lake shores in the very heart of Wordsworth Country.

Highlights: Fine mountain scenery and several sites, buildings and homes linked to the poet.

Option: None.

From Side Farm campsite walk along through Side Farm to reach Goldrill Bridge, as described at the end of the last stage. Walkers who have stayed overnight at the Patterdale Hotel or the youth hostel etc, should return to and cross the bridge. From here go through a kissing gate and walk along a footpath following the true right-hand bank (downstream) of the beck to where it joins the Side Farm access track quarter of a mile ahead. The large white building seen across the beck is the Patterdale Hotel, where the poet once stayed. >>

An ascent of Helvellyn from Patterdale was made in 1805 by William, Walter Scott and the chemist Humphrey Davy, when they climbed the mountain via the dizzying Striding Edge. The night before the journey William and Scott found lodgings at the Patterdale Hotel, an important coaching-inn in those days. The name Patterdale is believed by some to be a corruption of St Patrick's Dale.

>> Turn left along the farm track and at the main road turn

The Helvellyn range clothed in winter raiment, seen from Grizedale

right in the direction of Glenridding. Immediately before the bridge over Grizedale Beck turn left up the lane and follow this past Patterdale Hall, noting the sequoia tree just after this on the left. Sequoia is the generic name for the *Taxodiaceae* family of trees, which include the giant Californian redwoods. A number of these were introduced as an experiment at various locations throughout Britain during the last century.

At a junction where Home Farm lies straight on, follow the lane around to the right (signposted Helvellyn via Striding Edge) as it rises steeply uphill at first. After a steady climb, the way breaks out of the trees and becomes gentler as the gradient eases, giving views up Grizedale towards mighty Helvellyn and its neighbours.

When a junction is met, and Helvellyn is indicated off to the right, continue straight forward for Grizedale Tarn and Grasmere, the route as far as the tarn being coincident with a low-level option of the west-bound Coast to Coast Walk. Another junction is reached where a right turn crosses a bridge for Braesteads farmstead. Ignore this and continue straight forward along a bridleway. Very soon the last dwelling and the fertile lower reaches of the dale are left behind, and the steep ground on the left culminates in the summit of St Sunday Crag, which overshadows our route.

Ahead, the eastern aspect of the Helvellyn range opens up in all its craggy grandeur. The valley pinches in and the path begins its climb towards Grizedale Hause, creeping ever higher to reach Ruthwaite climbing hut. From here the trail contours up the valley passing beneath Spout Crag, Falcon Crag and Tarn Crag, three 'warty' toes that Dollywaggon Pike dips into the valley. This mountain probably derives its unusual but delightful name from the Old Norse *dolgr* for 'giant' and *veginn* meaning 'uplifted'. The opposite flank of the valley comprises St Sunday Crag and Fairfield with the frost-shattered Coffa Pike squeezed in between.

The path soon levels beyond Tarn Crag allowing walkers to catch their breath. Taking advantage of this respite before the final and steepest climb of the day, look for a boulder known as the Brothers Parting Stone away to the left of the path, just before reaching Grizedale Tarn. The location is marked by a metal sign. >>

It was beside the tarn here on 29 September 1805 that William saw his brother John for the last time, exchanging their farewells as John once more departed for the high seas. He had become captain of the *Earl of Abergavenny*, an East India Merchantman, possibly the most important ship in the fleet at the time. He wrote to William from Portsmouth immediately before embarking, and a few days later, on 5 February 1806, he perished when the ship sank off Portland Bill. William was devastated by the news and did not compose any new poetry for almost three months. He later wrote *Elegiac Verses, In Memory of My Brother John*, a few lines of which, in the 1880s, were inscribed into the large, squarish boulder a little way downstream from the outlet of Grizedale Tarn.

>> When the large cairn is reached beyond the Parting Stone take the path leading across to the outlet from the tarn, and from there follow a rising line above the lake to reach Grizedale Hause, the gap separating the hills of Fairfield and its neglected satellite, Seat Sandal. At this point, turn left and climb a path alongside a ruined wall, backward glances giving a bird's-eye view of the beautiful tarn. >>

King Dunmail, the last monarch of Cumbria, was defeated

The route along Grizedale, overshadowed by Dollywaggon Pike and the Helvellyn range

in AD945 by the Anglo-Saxon Edmund, King of Northumbria, who afterwards passed the land into the ownership of King Malcolm of the Scots. Legend states that after King Dunmail fell in battle at the pass of Dunmail, his helm was carried over nearby Seat Sandal and cast into the steely waters of Grizedale Tarn. Since then the warrior-bearers return each year over the shoulder of the mountain, raise the helm from its watery resting place and carry it back to the mound at the pass, beneath which 'tis said King Dunmail lies. The leader strikes the stones three times with his lance, to which there is a reply: 'Not yet, not yet, wait awhile, my warriors.' At this they melt into the mist and await the passing of another year. The stone cairn on Dunmail Raise is mentioned in *The Wagonner*:

> The horses cautiously pursue
> Their way, without mishap or fault;
> And now have reached that pile of stones,
> Heaped over brave King Dunmail's bones;
> He who had once supreme command,
> Last king of rocky Cumberland;
> His bones, and those of all his Power
> Slain here in a disastrous hour!

Fairfield is a mountain with a split personality, its craggy north-eastern face contrasting with its much gentler, grassy flanks to the south and west. It featured in the verse *To Joanna*, which deals with the mountain echo of Joanna's laugh – 'And Fairfield answered with a mountain tone'. When the evening light is seen from here Grizedale Tarn looks like a warrior's shield of burnished platinum.

>> From Grizedale Hause the way climbs very steeply for half a mile before there is any let-up in the gradient, until at last it levels out at the summit cairn. From here descend to the south-east for 250 yards following what is in fact the anti-clockwise circuit of the Fairfield Horseshoe Walk, bearing south-west down a broad, grassy ridge leading to Great Rigg.

Leaving the summit, continue as if heading for Rydal Fell, but after 300 yards a cairn marks where a less obvious path branches off to the right along a subsidiary grassy spur. Follow this through minor outcrops of fretted rock to reach a more massive outcrop called Stone Arthur, overlooking Grasmere and its host vale.

The angle increases as the path drops now towards the steep-sided Greenhead Gill. When a wall is met the path continues parallel to it then descends towards the gill, passing through lush bracken slopes until reaching a wall corner by a small wood. Turn left down the side of this using a path worn into a deeply incised groove.

The deep ravine of Greenhead Gill is where William searched out an isolated sheepfold that he wished to describe in his poem *Michael*. Overlooking the gill is Stone Arthur, a rocky outcrop that inspired further verse.

The steep descent is relieved by fine views across the valley to Helm Crag, a relatively minor summit that again featured in *The Wagonner*. The configuration of the rocks forming its modest top have inspired alternative visionary images of a Lion and Lamb and an Old Woman Playing an Organ, depending both on one's point of view and imagination.

At the gill turn right through a gate and down a metalled lane beside the stream to reach a T-junction and turn left. Within a few yards is another junction. Turning right at this point leads to the Swan Inn at the bottom of the hill, but bear left instead and, crossing Greenhead Gill, walk on down the lane between houses. Immediately on the right just before the lane takes a right-angled turn is a cottage called Ben Place. >>

Dove Cottage, home to William Wordsworth from 1799 to 1808

The Swan Inn features in *The Wagonner* and was the ale-house where Sir Walter Scott often retired for a tot of the hard stuff while staying at Dove Cottage with Wordsworth. Ben Place was the home of George Dawson, upon whom was modelled Oswald in *The Excursion* (vii.695–890). In this scene the Pastor relates tales of the deceased, and tells of the death of young Oswald, a veteran of the Napoleonic Wars, while dipping his father's sheep. William himself had attended the funeral and was deeply moved by the loss of the gallant young man.

>> Around the corner from Ben Place follow the lane down to the A591 by the Catholic church. Turn left and cross the road, within a few yards turning right along a farm track (public footpath). Walk down to and pass through a gate. Then, keeping a wall on your right initially, then a fence line, follow this to a kissing gate. Go through this and trace the fieldpath across lush meadows through three more gates.

After the third, walk forward for 30 yards then veer right between a schoolroom and the beck, down a tarmac lane and through the school playground to reach the road on the edge of Grasmere. Turn left and walk along the road to the junction at the A591. On the left here is a drinking-fountain erected in memory of the poet. Across the junction walk up the narrow lane leaving the main road at an angle, the group of buildings here known as Town End. >>

The most notable property here of course is Dove Cottage, home to the Wordsworths between 1799 and 1808, after which Thomas de Quincey, a family friend and the so-called 'Opium-eater', took over the tenancy for the next 28 years.

Before it became a family home, Dove Cottage had once been an inn, the Dove and Olive Branch. It was here at Dove Cottage that William arguably enjoyed his most creative years, writing among other works *To a Butterfly*, *The Green Linnet*, *The Brothers*, *Michael*, the *Lucy* poems, *Nutting*, *The Rainbow*, *Written with a Pencil upon a Stone* and his famous *Immortality Ode*. The year 1807 saw the publication of *Poems in Two Volumes*, which contained such gems as *My Heart Leaps Up*, *To the Daisy*, *Daffodils*, *Ode to Duty* and *Among all Lovely Things*.

Today Dove Cottage and the nearby museum, both managed by the Dove Cottage Trust, enjoy a steady stream of visitors all year round. Almost opposite the cottage, a little way up the lane, was Sykeside, where the Fishers lived; Molly Fisher was employed as a servant, and her sister-in-law, Agnes, was described in *The Excursion* (vi.765–77). Below Dove Cottage down the lane was the Ashburners' house, Peggy and Thomas being very close friends of the Wordsworth family.

>> With Dove Cottage and Museum on the left, continue up the hill to a small pond beyond which is a junction (signposted White Moss and Ambleside) opposite How Top Farm. Turn right here and stroll along the road to a sharp left-hand bend. >>

Some 100 yards before this is the site of John's Grove, and between here and the bend is the site of the Wishing Gate. The Wishing Gate was the subject of a poem of the same name. From here views can be obtained towards the steep pass of Dunmail Raise, over which Benjamin in the *The Wagonner* struggled to coax his horse-drawn wain. John's Grove was just across the road and down a little from the site of the gate. Naming natural features after friends and family was William's way, or so it would appear, of ensuring that a personal life force lived on after death.

>> From the bend the road winds through mixed deciduous woodland and rock outcrops across White Moss Common, eventually turning downhill towards its junction with the A591 at the National Trust carpark. Just before this on the left beside the road is a large boulder known to the Wordsworths as Glow-worm Rock. At the junction walk through the carpark and along a footpath parallel with the road, crossing a small brook to a telephone box. >>

Glow-worm Rock was the source of inspiration for three poems, *Inscribed upon a Rock* and the later *The Primrose and the Rock*. Another verse, *The Star and the Glow-worm* was also suggested by this same location. Before the present road was routed around by Bainriggs, it was once the main route from Ambleside to Keswick, and the Wagonner would have had to pass this way.

>> Immediately beyond the telephone box, walk left in front of the entrance to the Coach House and follow a footpath uphill alongside a boisterous stream. After 30 yards the stony way splits by a waterfall. Take the right branch and, still climbing, follow this to eventually reach two gates. Ignore the right-hand one and proceed straight ahead between two walls until a bridleway is intersected in front of a house.

Bear right to a gate from where there are fine views across Rydal Water to Loughrigg Fell. Easy, level going now continues through mixed woodland tracing a bridleway that was often used by the Wordsworths when walking between Rydal Mount and Grasmere. The way soon becomes a switchback trail beneath the wooded heights of Nab Scar. Consisting principally of oak cover, it is thronged with birdlife and redolent of the poem *The Oak and the Broom*.

Soon the path opens up along a pleasing terrace walk with the lake beckoning as Rydal village is approached. As you near the latter, it is easy to understand why the Wordsworths were so much in raptures over the scenery of this pleasant vale; out of sight of the A591 below, the scene has changed little since those romantic times.

Just before entering the village, immediately before the corner wall of Rydal Mount, the path passes a pretentious spring known as Nab Well. Hardly inspiring today, and failing to meet the literal concept of Wordsworth's fountain, this resurgence was nevertheless the eponymous subject of a verse. Go through a gate just beyond the spring and along the walled bridleway to a second one. Over the wall to the right can be glimpsed some of the glory that make the gardens one of the highlights of a visit to Rydal Mount. Much of the landscaping was carried out by William himself.

When the metalled lane is met turn downhill passing the entrance to Rydal Mount. A few yards beyond, a turning to the left leads to Rydal Hall. About 100 yards along here is the Rambler's Teashop and excellent views of Rydal Beck from the bridge spanning its boisterous course. Rydal is a small but pretty hamlet – hardly large enough to warrant being called a village – retired among trees at the very focus of everything Wordsworthian. >>

The distinctive round chimneys of the cottages in Rydal, and indeed elsewhere in the Lakes, are due in no small part to the poet's influence. William believed chimneys constructed square part way up and round from there on upwards were more aesthetically pleasing. The old high 'road' out of Rydal passing Nab Well was popular with William and Dorothy, and a number of poems were inspired by the environs.

The move to Rydal was made possible by virtue of the increased affluence that came with William's appointment as Distributor of Stamps for Westmoreland. As a result, perhaps, of his new-found affluence, many important visitors were received at the Mount, including Sir Walter Scott, Harriett Martineau, Keats and Benjamin Haydon.

In the late 16th century the house was a yeoman farmer's cottage, later added to in the 18th century, and then bought by one Ford North in 1803 who gave it its present name. This apparently reflects the fact that an earthen mound raised by Viking settlers was situated towards the front of the house. The property was later sold to Lady Fleming of Rydal Hall, from whom the Wordsworths were subsequently to let the house.

It is entirely due to the foresight of William's great-great-granddaughter, Mary Henderson (née Wordsworth), that Rydal Mount was acquired and opened to the public. The interior evokes life in the early 19th century and contains many period pieces, as well as paintings of the family and their friends. The Wordsworths moved into Rydal Mount in 1813 and here William stayed for the remainder of his days. It was an imposing house with extensive gardens that appear today much as they were after being landscaped and planted by William.

>> Continue down through Rydal towards the main road at the foot of the hill. Just before the junction is St Mary's Church. Turn right through the gate and walk beside the church through a gate at the back to enter Dora's Field. Immediately the path divides. Take the right-hand fork and walk along to the top of some stone steps close to the gate into the gardens of Rydal Mount.

Go down the steps and follow the lower path left to reach the gate at the point of entry. Return through the churchyard and turn right then right again along the main road at the bottom. After about 60 yards take off left along a footpath opposite the Glen Rothay Restaurant. Cross the footbridge over the Rothay and bear right along a well-beaten path beside the river and heading for the lake to reach a kissing gate. The margins of the lake in early summer are coloured by marsh marigolds and waterlilies. >>

St Mary's Church was built by Lady Fleming of nearby Rydal Hall. The structure is of no particular architectural interest but it does have some attractive stained-glass windows. The Wordsworths went to church here and William acted as chapel warden for a while. In the spring of 1850 the family prayed for William as he lay on his deathbed, their pew being the one on the front left, facing the pulpit. The Glen Rothay Restaurant incorporates Ivy Cottage, where William's brother Christopher stayed for a while.

Dora's Field was known in Wordsworth's day as the Rash. In late spring the sloping enclosure is a carpet of wild daffodils, and in early summer is taken over by the blooms of bluebells and ramsons. When it was thought that the family would have to vacate Rydal Mount, William purchased this field as a potential building plot in 1826. In the event the crisis passed and his tenure remained secure, but some time later he gave the field to his daughter Dora, after whom it is still known today. Ownership of the field passed to the National Trust in 1933. The enclosure still contains two inscriptions by Wordsworth. One may be found on a rock above some steps near to the gate to Rydal Mount. Walkers might care to search for the second.

Wordsworth is estimated to have walked around 180,000 miles during his long lifetime, but nowhere is the sense of following in the great bard's footsteps more pronounced than when wandering the paths around both Rydal and Grasmere, notably on Loughrigg Terrace, perhaps the most famous footpath in the district.

>> At the kissing gate the path enters the Rydal Woods Access Area, a pleasant woodland in which will be seen the white star-like flowers of stitchwort as well as carpets of bluebells. Just beyond the second kissing gate the path divides. Turn along the right-hand branch on an open-aspect path that has views across the lake of Nab Cottage and the overshadowing Nab Scar. >>

Rydal Water is a naturally serene body of water broken by three islands and overlooked to the south by Loughrigg Fell. Its eastern extremity, Lanty Scar, was known in the poet's day as Holme Scar. One of his poems refers to the outcrop as Aerial Rock. Heron Island, the largest islet of Rydal Water, furnished the inspiration and location for two poems, *The Wild Duck's Nest* and *Inscription Written with a Slate Pencil*.

Nab Cottage was once an 18th-century yeoman farmer's cottage, and was later where Hartley Coleridge, son of Wordsworth's friend, Samuel Taylor Coleridge, spent his last 11 years. Before that it was home to Peggy Simpson, a farmer's daughter with whom the Wordsworth family friend, Thomas de Quincey, fell in love.

>> Almost directly opposite Nab Cottage the path begins a gentle climb beside a wall and is signposted Grasmere and Red Bank. This soon levels out once again, still beside the wall, then beneath Ewe Crag crosses some stepping-stones and veers right by a ruined barn and alongside a small wood. The way climbs to the right then the left to join another path by a settle.

At this point a path takes off right for Grasmere Lake, while our route, the bridleway, takes off left along Loughrigg Terrace, where the poet set the finale in his lengthy work, *The Excursion*. Our way traverses across the slopes of Loughrigg Fell giving easy walking and wonderful views across Grasmere towards Helm Crag, Seat Sandal, Fairfield and Dunmail Raise. >>

Dunmail Raise, the highest point of the road pass between Grasmere and Wythburn, was known in Wordsworth's day simply as Rays. Where the two carriageways divide at the summit, a large cairn can be seen. It is said to be the resting-place of King Dunmail, but equally plausibly it could simply be a frontier marker between tenth-century Strathclyde and England. Seat Sandal rising to its right (eastern) flank was referred to as 'Fond lover of Clouds' in *The Wagonner*.

>> The path heads for Red Bank across bracken-covered slopes highlighted in early summer with patches of bluebells. The sharp-eyed may also spot examples of the fly-eating butterwort (*Pinguicula vulgaris*), the squat rosette of green leaves preferring moist ground and in June sending out a short stem terminating in a solitary blue, jewel-like flower.

The rising trail eventually meets a wall where another path joins at a tangent from the left. Cross a small beck before bearing right through a gate. After this proceed straight forward, ignoring a path on the right for Grasmere, and 50 yards later veering right at the fork shortly meeting and turning down the Red Bank road. Rising above to the left are the slopes of Hammerscar. >>

Hammerscar above Red Bank is where the young William, while still a pupil at Hawkshead school, first gazed upon the vale of Grasmere and sensed it was a special place where he would one day spend part of his life. The view was referred to in his unfinished work, *The Recluse*. As with all the natural features about his home, William and his sister revelled in the sublime beauty of Grasmere, having picnics on its solitary island and here writing a poem on one of the stones of a barn-like building.

>> Within only a few paces take the footpath left (sign-posted Grasmere), which contours above the road to enter Red Bank Woods at a kissing gate. A pleasant trail follows for about quarter of a mile amid vernal woodland dotted with wild flowers and ringing to the call of secretive birdlife. With luck you might hear the green woodpecker, its distinctive call resembling a guffawing laugh.

At another gate a path is intersected coming from Elter-water and Langdale. Turn right here, along a narrow, stony lane descending beside the edge of Nicholas Wood. The path is rough underfoot and commands the walker's attention if a twisted ankle is to be avoided, but distractions come in the form of the occasional glimpse of Grasmere lake with Great Rigg forming a backdrop.

The track becomes a metalled lane soon merging with the Red Bank road once again. Turn left for Grasmere some three-quarters of a mile distant. At the outskirts of the village, across some pastures to the left, can be seen the large house of Allan Bank nestling at the hem of a wood with Helm Crag rising behind. At the junction by the Dale Lodge Hotel carry on forward, passing the information centre on the right to reach a T-junction opposite the church. >>

When Allan Bank was built by a Liverpool family, the Crumps, it caused a great deal of local contention, not least from the Wordsworths themselves, who were very aware of matters of architectural taste. Quite ironically, however, Allan Bank would become their home between 1808 and 1811, shared occasionally by Coleridge and at one time with as many as 13 friends, family and relations who would some-times stay for months at a stretch.

The church is dedicated to St Oswald and remains today much as it was in William's life, when he described it in his lengthy itinerary poem, *The Excursion*. Then it had an earthen floor, which gave rise to the rush-bearing ceremony still main-tained to this day. At that time rushes and flowers were used to cover the floor, and were replaced each year on St Oswald's Day. Children taking part were treated to helpings of Gras-mere's famous gingerbread. Today the tradition takes place on the Saturday nearest St Oswald's Day (5 August).

Though the oldest parts of the church date from the 13th century, the structure is far from architecturally outstanding. Inside is a marble memorial to Wordsworth above and to the left of the altar. Fragments of stone built into the fabric are thought to date from Anglo-Saxon times. While strolling in the churchyard it is worth noting that the yew trees seen there today were each planted by the hand of William.

In the far right-hand corner of the churchyard can be found the graves of William and his wife Mary, his sister Dorothy, his daughter, Dora Quillinan, and Hartley Coleridge. Besides the Wordsworth family graves, Grasmere is also the resting place of Sir John Richardson (1787–1865), the famous explorer who served on the Arctic expeditions of Parry and Franklin.

>> Turn left out of the junction, cross the road and walk as far as Sarah Nelson's gingerbread shop. Turn right through the lychgate into the churchyard and take the path to the left (signposted to Wordsworth's grave), following this through the churchyard to the road at the opposite gate. The Rectory is across the way from the church. >>

The Rectory (Wordsworth's home from 1811 to 1813) was considered a gloomy residence. It was the focus of a sad period in the poet's life, for his daughter Catherine died at the age of three after a lengthy illness, to be followed six months later by the death of six-year-old Thomas who had suffered an attack of pneumonia. The poem *Surprised by Joy* reflects William's sadness at the loss. It was penned while he was still living at the Rectory, but the second tragedy forced a move when looking out of the window each day onto the churchyard where their little ones were laid to rest became too much to bear.

Grasmere is noted for its fell races, its gingerbread, Cumberland wrestling, the rush-bearing ceremony and, not least, its Wordsworth connections. Indeed Grasmere vies with Rydal as the very heart of what could be regarded as Wordsworth Country. Adjacent to the lychgate of the church is a tiny gingerbread shop. Until 1854 it was the village schoolhouse where the poet's son, John, had lessons, and where for a brief period in 1811 William taught the local children. The places in and around the village furnished a setting in *The Excursion* and also inspired other works, for instance *Home at Grasmere*, *A Farewell* and *An Evening Walk*.

>> Walkers seeking a bed for the night will find ample

guest-house or hotel accommodation in the village. To continue the route and camp wild or stay at either of the local YHA hostels, turn left out of the church gate and cross the bridge. Walk along the road out of the village, but just before leaving the latter take a footpath (fingerpost) to the left, through the Church of England Primary School grounds.

Walk across the playground in front of the main building passing between two further classrooms. Just beyond these ignore a way bearing right between railings and a wall, and instead turn left beside the river to a gate. Go through this and trace an obvious farm track forward across lush meadows. Views of Helm Crag can be seen on the left, the Lion and the Lamb summit rocks prominent, and the rocky eminence of Stone Arthur visible on a skyline immediately in front.

In a little less than half a mile, and three kissing gates later, the path meets the A591. Turn left here and left again within just a few yards, along a footpath (fingerpost) between a fence and a wall. When the road is met just beyond Riversdale House, turn left over the bridge, then pick up the footpath to the right almost immediately opposite the Rothay Garden Hotel.

The continuing way passes through Butterlip Howe, skirting around the base of the small knoll on its northern side. A path leads to its wooded head where a settle offers an opportunity to sit and contemplate Arthur's Seat, seen across the dale up through the tree cover.

When the Easedale road is met at the far side of Butterlip Howe, go through the gate and turn left to reach the Butterlip Howe hostel within a few paces, or turn to the right to continue up the road for Thorney How hostel and to camp in the upper valley (in both cases follow the directions for Easedale Tarn in Day 8).

William could be regarded as one of the first conservationists, for in 1810 he attempted to purchase the land at Butterlip Howe to prevent it falling into the wrong hands and being ruined. It was a favourite haunt of William and Dorothy, the latter referring to it often in her journal. It has now been protected for all time under the management of the National Trust.

USEFUL INFORMATION

Accommodation: A choice of hotels, guest-houses and B&Bs in Grasmere. B&B at the Swan Inn.

Camping: No official campsite in Grasmere, but wild camping is possible near Easedale Tarn. Those feeling really fit could continue into Langdale and use the campsite here (see Useful Information for Day 8).

Youth Hostel: Thorney How hostel. Tel: (015394) 35591 and Butterlip Howe hostel. Tel: (015394) 35316.

Transport: Service No.555 (Lakeslink) linking Windermere, Ambleside, Rydal, Grasmere, Wythburn Church and Keswick.

Supplies: Village shops.

Refreshments: Rambler's Teashop, Rydal. Pubs and cafés in Grasmere.

Tourist Information: Red Bank Road, Grasmere. Tel: (015394) 35245.

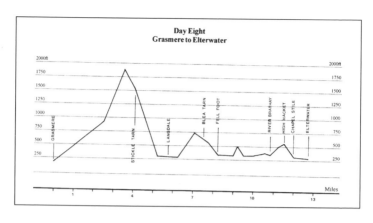

Day Eight
Grasmere to Elterwater

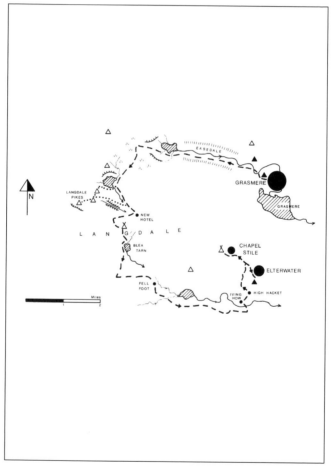

DAY 8
Grasmere to Elterwater

SUMMARY
Distance: 12.75 miles.
Total Ascent: 2,601 feet (793 metres).
Expected Duration: 4–5 hours.
Map: 1:25000 Outdoor Leisure Series sheet Nos.6, 7.
Terrain and Difficulty: An inter-valley route crossing rugged
  mountain terrain followed by easier going in second half
  of day. Crosses exposed fells between Grasmere and
  Langdale.
Highlights: The famous Langdale Pikes, mountain tarns and
  scenery that featured in *The Excursion*. Several sites
  connected with Wordsworth.
Option: Ascent of Langdale Pikes (add 1.5 hours).

Those who have spent the night in Grasmere centre must now
leave the village by following the directions from the church
for Butterlip Howe as described at the end of the previous
stage. Then, turning right beyond Butterlip Howe, walk up the
road for Easedale. From Butterlip Howe hostel turn right, up
the Easedale road.

Walk along here to a point just before the carpark, turning
left through a gate and right along a footpath parallel to but
avoiding part of the road. When the latter is rejoined continue
along the lane, passing the entrance to Thorney How youth
hostel after 100 yards. Continue forward along the lane
noting that hereabouts the beck over the wall on the left flows
in a wooded hollow which was known to Wordsworth as
Emma's Dell (Emma being one of the names William
employed when writing about his sister Dorothy).

The road soon bends to the right. Just on this curve our
route bears left over a footbridge to pick up a path signposted
for Easedale Tarn. The obvious wide track heads up the dale
with Helm Crag rising to the right, its wooded flanks at this
point known as Lancrigg, and which was one of the

Wordsworth household's favourite places to walk. >>

It was common in the poet's time for travellers to have pointed out to them the summit rocks of Helm Crag which, depending on the point from which they are viewed, resemble an Old Woman Playing an Organ (viewed from Easedale) or the Lion and the Lamb (seen from Dunmail Raise). The summit may be easily reached in about an hour by a steeply winding path from Lancrigg. Easedale was one of the Wordsworths' favourite places, especially a terrace walk at Lancrigg overshadowed by Helm Crag.

The Wordsworths sometimes called Easedale the Black Quarter since it seemed, to them at least, that much of the worst weather approached from here. Many of the poet's more famous works were supposedly composed along the banks of the clear brook that meanders through this pleasant valley. He wrote a great deal of *The Prelude* at Lancrigg, elsewhere composing *Poems on the Naming of Places* and *It was an April morning*.

>> Apart from the Loughrigg Terrace walk and Martindale, nowhere is the presence of the poet felt more strongly than in this pleasant, almost hanging side valley. After a mere ten minutes' walk from the footbridge a footpath turns off left through a gate, but the main route is forward. >>

Away to the left a little beyond this point, a white-painted cottage situated on Blindtarn Gill had melancholy associations for Wordsworth and local villagers. It belonged to Sarah and George Green who, on their return from a farm sale in Langdale, perished on high ground after losing the path in a sudden snowstorm. Their grave can be seen in Grasmere churchyard. The Wordsworths helped relieve the plight of their orphaned children.

In very wet weather the dale is almost awash with water, the powerful stream from its secluded mountain tarn tumbling noisily down the waterfall today known as Sour Milk Gill, and which was known to Dorothy Wordsworth as Churn Milk Force. Beyond the cataract the beck crosses rough ground scattered with juniper bushes.

>> The path claws its way up the hillside beside Sour Milk Gill and onwards into an upper basin embracing the secluded Easedale Tarn, a body of water mentioned by William in his Lakeland guide and believed by him to be one of the finest in all the land. Just before the upstream limit of the tarn take the

more obvious right-hand path branching off at a junction marked by a cairn, and follow its rising line as it slips through the gap between Eagle Crag and Slapestone Edge. The way climbs beside a stream to where it divides beneath Belles Knott. Don't cross the stream here, a footpath heading for Codale Tarn, but instead keep to the left-hand route (cairned) which continues to the watershed.

When the top of the pass is reached ignore the path sneaking off to the right, and instead walk ahead on a bearing of 200 degrees to a cairn surmounting a hummock 30 yards in front. From here bear off at 160 degrees tracing a vague hint of a downhill path. The spangled surface of Stickle Tarn soon comes into view and the way then becomes clearer as it loses height towards the outfall of the lake. When placid the surface of the latter mirrors the grey cliff of Pavey Arc rising above the far shore, the obvious diagonal feature ascending right to left across the face being Jack's Rake, a scrambling route of some notoriety.

The upper Langdale valley has much to commend it and in spite of tourism pressures has managed to avoid much of the clamour, development and bad taste that usually accompany the holiday crowds. To ramble here beside Stickle Tarn, on the Langdale Pikes and beside Dungeon Ghyll Force, is a pleasure enhanced by the feeling of actually experiencing the natural drama enshrined in Wordsworth's verse.

A dam marks the outflow from the tarn. At this point the walker faces two possibilities: to continue directly into the valley following the directions as for Dungeon Ghyll Hotel Direct (that is, a descent beside Mill Gill), or to cross the stepping-stones and the dam and continue, as below, taking advantage of the option climbing Langdale's sentinel peaks. The famous Pikes are probably the most photographed and easily recognised skyline of the whole district.

LANGDALE PIKES OPTION
Leave the dam and walk forward taking the well-worn trail climbing from the south-western shore of the tarn, up between Pavey Arc and the northern side of Harrison Stickle. The well-engineered trail soon becomes a scree scramble, but only to the point where a ridge path is joined coming from the right, from Pavey Arc. Here the going eases somewhat.

Turn left at this point and within a few yards take the left option when the way divides, very soon gaining the rock-writhed head of Harrison Stickle. The continuing path picks its way down the western side of the peak to where it splits yet again. Ignore the left branch to continue straight ahead on a path benefiting from a series of chunky stepping-stones crossing the boggy Harrison Combe, heading for Pike O'Stickle.

At the base of the final dome of this peak the route to the summit takes off close to the head of a precipitous scree gully. A point part way down the latter marks the site where a Neolithic axe factory of national importance was discovered in 1947. Axe blanks or roughs originating here have been identified throughout the country by archaeologists. The climb to the summit is a partial scramble but presents little difficulty. The views from its modest summit will compensate even the most timid walker. >>

The two principal peaks of this group, Pike O'Stickle and Harrison Stickle, were the much admired 'companions' of the character referred to by Wordsworth as the Solitary in *The Excursion* (ii.692–96). The 'lusty twins' can be seen to advantage from across Langdale, beside the fine Blea Tarn. Stickle Tarn was where he imagined an echo, described in the same poem (iv.402–12).

>> To continue down into the valley, retrace your steps to the far (east) side of the Harrison Combe stepping-stones and turn right along an obvious footpath skirting the craggy south face of Harrison Stickle. This superb route represents a true mountain trail, albeit short-lived, that clings to the steep shoulder high above the echoing depths of Dungeon Ghyll. In the wooded lower reaches of this narrow ravine is secreted a waterfall that was the subject of a poem by Wordsworth, *The Idle Shepherd-Boys*.

The narrow, descending trail demands care and attention, but the magnificent vista across the valley is a constant distraction, with views into the valley and across this towards Blea Tarn, Pike O'Blisco and Crinkle Crags. The panorama stretches away to the south, the Furness Fells leading the eye towards the distant, pale blue ribbon of sea at Morecambe Bay.

Soon the way meets a stile where a path takes off to the right, fords a brook and heads steeply back uphill. Ignore this to cross the stile and follow the wall down to a gate in the corner with a bridleway branching off to the right. Turn left through the gate and walk straight ahead beside the wall, ignoring a gate on the right within a few yards. Continue downhill towards the trees, where the way merges with the direct route joining from the left coming from Stickle Tarn. Turn right here and follow directions from this point as for Langdale Continuation, as below.

DUNGEON GHYLL HOTEL DIRECT

Cross the stepping-stones and dam. An obvious but steep path on the left here descends beside an impetuous stream directly into Langdale at the New Dungeon Ghyll Hotel. The way down is rocky underfoot and the walker is drawn ever downwards by the turbulent cataract. Eventually, and within sight of the hotel, the path passes through a wall and forks. Take the right-hand branch and go through the gate to reach and cross a footbridge. Continue down the true right-hand bank to the point, about 170 yards later, where the Langdale Pikes option joins from the right.

LANGDALE CONTINUATION

Walk forward between two small woods to where the path shortly splits. Take the left branch, passing through a hole in the wall just ahead, then turn right down to a gate beside the hotel. Once through the gate bear right, through the Stickle Barn beer garden and a gate leading to the main valley carpark.

At the far side of the carpark take a footpath giving access to pastureland at a gate, and go straight forward passing in front of a farmhouse to trace a track around to the left to find a stile and gate. Through this, turn right across a bridge and then sharp left, walking forward parallel to the streambed on your left, eventually to reach two stiles in a wall corner.

Cross this and the stile a few steps ahead then turn left and head for a gate hole in the far wall. From there follow a path marked with yellow direction arrows beneath the craggy heights of the Pikes. When the path passes in front of the Old Dungeon Ghyll Hotel, head for a gate in the far corner of the paddock. Go through this, cross the lane, and go through a second gate immediately in front. Bear half left through a gate and across an arched bridge to reach the valley road.

Walk forward along this to where it turns sharp right just after the bridge. Turn left (signposted public footpath) into the

The William Wordsworth Way passes through woodland at Blea Tarn, between Great and Little Langdale

Langdale campsite and, keeping to the wall on your right, trace this around to the right to where it ends. Walk forward through a kissing gate and another gate just a few steps in front. Climb over the rise and pass through a small conifer plantation.

Once clear of the trees, the way ascends steeply to where it meets the minor road to Little Langdale. There are excellent views from here into the valley head of Langdale, known as Mickleden. The path continues forward parallel with the road for a further 250 yards to a ladder stile by a cattle grid. Cross the stile and the road and walk left through a gap in the dry-stone wall to follow an obvious trail heading south for Blea Tarn.

Easy, level walking contours through pleasant woods and along the west side of Blea Tarn. Across the valley can be seen a solitary whitewashed cottage and, rising directly behind this, the knobbly hill of Lingmoor Fell, both of which played a part in *The Excursion*.

At the south end of the lake don't cross the bridge, but instead go forward through a gate and continue along a path that cuts a dash through slopes heavily festooned with bracken. The forward view is dominated by Wetherlam.

When the Wrynose Pass road is met, turn left and walk down past the obvious rock tower of Castle Howe and Fell Foot Farm. About 50 yards after the farm turn right over a packhorse bridge and along a stony lane leading through Bridge End. Immediately after this continue left along a walled track contouring left then climbing over a shoulder of the fellside giving good views of the Langdale Pikes.

>> After climbing directly out of Great Langdale by way of Lingmoor Tarn, the Poet and the Wanderer in *The Excursion* gaze down upon a tiny urn-like valley in which can be seen a solitary dwelling and a nearby lake. The house is Blea Tarn farmhouse. The tarn is perhaps the best known of those bearing this name, because of its connections with *The Excursion* (ll.327–48).

Near Fell Foot beside the road a flat-topped mound marked on the map as Thing Mound may represent a Norse meeting place, or moot, where Viking settlers gathered and important decisions were given assent by a show of weapons (the Norse *vapnatak* from which the English 'wapentake' is derived). Despite the fact that most of the Pastor's role in *The Excursion* was set in Grasmere, it was Fell Foot that was the location for the Parsonage.

>> In a little over quarter of a mile from Bridge End ignore the right branch at a parting of the ways. Continue down Little Langdale to eventually enter a walled lane through a

The Langdale Pikes, Wordsworth's 'Lusty Twins', from the bridleway near Fell Foot in Little Langdale

gate. Proceed past High Hall Garth, some disused quarry tips and the farmstead of Low Hall Garth, then along the continuing lane. About 130 yards down this, a path leads off left over a stile to the ancient Slater Bridge, an ideal place to halt for a spot of lunch. The stones from which this tiny bridge is built are heavily worn by the passage of packhorse traffic, once a common feature of the Lakes in bygone times.

Continue down the track to a more modern structure spanning the Brathay. Ignore this and the path continuing along the riverbank, and instead turn to the right. Where the track divides allow the left branch to lead you onto the metalled lane through Stang End towards High Park House. Just before this, pick up a footpath left over a stile. This is a public right of way though there is no obvious trace upon the ground. Descend to the wooded banks of the river, crossing a stile in the right-hand corner of the field. After negotiating the stepping-stones over the river climb an overgrown path to the road and turn left.

After approximately 200 yards turn right into the entrance of Iving Howe (signposted to Elterwater) and cross a cattle grid. Then, opposite the house, veer right over a stile adjacent to a gate. Beyond this, a vague outline of a path is traced left, right, then left again between some rock outcrops (waymarked with occasional white arrows). Beyond the rocks the way extends beside a wall to reach a gate within a few yards.

Continue forward and climb to another gate in the wall corner. Ignore the path off to the right (signed to Elterwater) and instead go forward through the gate and walk uphill towards a farm (High Hackett) partly hidden in trees on the hill, but after 60 yards or so veer left along a vague hint of a path going through a gate hole (some yellow waymarking arrows). >>

Iveing Howe (or Iving Howe as it is spelt today) was purchased by William prior to the 1818 Westmoreland Parliamentary Election so that he could divide and distribute small plots of land to supporters of Lowther in the forthcoming election, and thus give them a freeholder's right to vote. As Distributor of Stamps (the equivalent of a Civil Service position), William was, of course, treading on thin ice by involving himself in election campaigns.

The house at High Hacket is where John and Betty Youdell lived and put up the Wordsworth offspring when they had been ailing in 1810. William also employed the Youdells' daughter, Sarah, as the family maid at their Allan Bank home.

>> Beyond the gate walk forward keeping to the wall on your right, but when this curves away to the right continue forward keeping the same line across the rise to find and cross a step stile in the far wall. Cross this and walk forward on a bearing of 120 degrees to find a gate hole in the far corner of the pasture. Once through this, walk forward a few yards to intersect a path coming from the left. Turn right along this and at a kissing gate meet and turn right along the wide track leading to Dale End.

Just where Sawrey Woods are entered, follow a bridleway left (fingerpost) through broadleaf woodland cover, over a rise and downhill passing disused quarry tips and beneath Yew Crag. A wider track is intersected just in front of a house. Turn right along this, then left at a metalled lane to reach the continuation of the bridleway off on the right a few yards later.

The route lies through a large slate quarry complex and is waymarked with blue arrows at strategic points on posts and the corners of buildings. Just beyond the main buildings at the eastern end of the site, the bridleway turns off and descends to the left of a cottage. The way passes through a curious walled cutting and then for about 200 yards runs alongside Langdale Beck to a bridge.

To reach the youth hostel (a further half-mile) turn right here, otherwise cross the bridge for the campsite and accommodation in Chapel Stile. At the road end turn left and then, just after the Wainwright Inn and before entering the village, turn left (fingerpost) to follow a wide track for 200 yards to a metalled lane. >>

The village of Chapel Stile has avoided the modern development that has robbed neighbouring Elterwater of much of its character. Its Holy Trinity Church, erected in native stone and proudly towering over the village, is where the Poet and friends in *The Excursion* (vii.541–45) witness a wain bearing a huge oak. Moreover, the place is the subject of *Epitaph in the Church-Yard of Langdale, Westmoreland*, which Wordsworth carved on the tombstone of the Reverend Owen Lloyd.

>> Turn left and pass Thrang Farm on its right to reach a gate. Here a narrow, walled path is entered and followed to its junction with a track at a sweeping bend. Turn left along this to reach the campsite.

Walkers heading for the youth hostel or accommodation in Elterwater must continue from the bridge over Langdale Beck, down its true right bank. This is a pleasant stretch of riverside path – or would be but for the timeshare apartments clustered on the far bank. The track eventually merges with a metalled road by the yawning mouth of a disused underground stone quarry (DANGER: KEEP OUT). Turn left along the road here, tracing this for a further quarter-mile or so to a T-junction in Elterwater village. Here turn left over the bridge into the village, or right to reach the hostel, a few minutes' walk further down the road on the right.

Elterwater village was once a centre of gunpowder manufacture until the close of the First World War when production ceased. The factory was sited on the true left bank of Langdale Beck where the timeshare complex now stands. The lake itself forms an irregular body of water where the River Brathay has its confluence with Langdale Beck. The lake and its vegetated shoreline provide valuable habitats for birds such as coot and mallard.

USEFUL INFORMATION

Accommodation: Guest-houses, hotels and B&Bs in Chapel Stile and Elterwater.

Camping: Great Langdale campsite, near the Old Dungeon Ghyll. £3/night/person. Open all year. Shop and full facilities. Baysbrown campsite, Chapel Stile. £1.80/night/person. WC and sink but no shower. Also B&B at the farm.

Bunkbarn: Sticklebarn Bunkbarn. Tel: (015394) 37356. Drying room, showers/WC. Not self-catering, but meals available in nearby Sticklebarn Tavern.

Youth Hostel: Elterwater hostel. Tel: (015394) 37245.

Transport: Service No.516 links Ambleside to Dungeon Ghyll (Langdale) via Skelwith Bridge, Elterwater and Chapel Stile. Also linking Kendal and Windermere (Sundays).

Supplies: One or two small shops in Elterwater and a co-op in Chapel Stile (sells camping Gaz and Coleman gas cartridges).

Refreshments: New Dungeon Ghyll pub in Great Langdale and pubs in Chapel Stile and Elterwater.

DAY 9
Elterwater to High Cross

SUMMARY

Distance: 9.75 miles (to High Cross YHA hostel). Add 0.75 mile to Troutbeck Bridge for village centre hotels, B&Bs.

Total Ascent: 1,115 feet (340 metres).

Expected Duration: 3 hours.

Map: 1:25000 Outdoor Leisure Series sheet No.7.

Terrain and Difficulty: Easy walking mostly between the 100 and 700 feet contours.

Highlights: Skelwith Force, Loughrigg Tarn and unexpected views of Windermere.

Option: None.

CHAPEL STILE START

From the campsite or village centre retrace yesterday's steps back to the bridge over the beck and follow the instructions for Elterwater in the previous section. From Elterwater youth hostel turn left up the road to the bridge in the village. Cross this then take the footpath signposted on the right for Skelwith Bridge, continuing along a well-made pathway between the stream and the valley-bottom meadows. The route lies alongside Great Langdale Beck, a clear-flowing stream originating from many sources above Mickleden, high among a knot of England's finest mountains. >>

Pleasant broadleaf woodlands give occasional glimpses over the placid Elterwater, a local widening of the River Brathay where it meets Great Langdale Beck. It is a serene, almost magical place, believed by some to derive its name from a Scandinavian word for 'swan'. It is a rather secretive stretch of water partially hidden by trees and reedy margins. The footpath along its northern side is shared by the Cumbria Way long-distance footpath.

>> At a gate, more open country is entered and crossed for the remaining half-mile to where the way meets the B5343. Forsake the road in favour of a stroll along the continuing

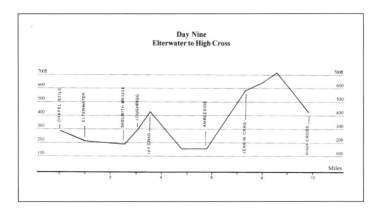

Day Nine
Elterwater to High Cross

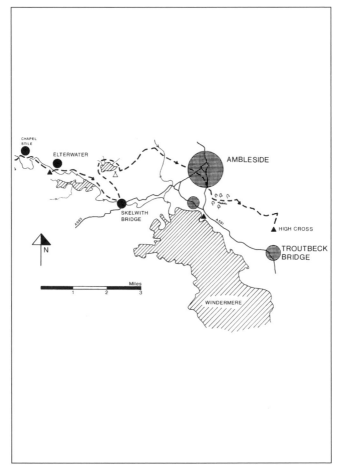

path, parallel to the road. Just before the river slides beneath Skelwith Bridge, gravity urges the Brathay over Skelwith Force.

At the village follow the right of way straight ahead through a slate merchant's yard to a lane. Turn left by the riverside picnic site to reach the main road. Turn left and at the junction turn left again. After 60 yards take the footpath (fingerpost and stile) on the right, immediately opposite the Talbot Inn.

Walk forward beside the wall for a few paces then head upwards into the tree cover. The path climbs steeply through a holiday-cabin complex and is clearly marked (look for the yellow direction arrows on posts). At the top of the hill the tarmac ends and the cabins are left behind in favour of a continuing path passing through a young pine wood to a step stile. At this point Loughrigg Tarn may be glimpsed away to the north-east. >>

Loughrigg Tarn is an idyllic little lake referred to by Wordsworth as Diana's Looking-glass in his *Epistle to Sir G.H. Beaumont*, friend and benefactor of the Wordsworth household. Placid more often than not and forming a perfect mirror for Langdale's 'Lusty Twins', the tarn makes a fine sight when backed by the famed Pikes.

>> Negotiate the stile and walk downhill through bracken to Crag Head House to reach the road at High Loughrigg Fold. Turn left along the road and at the foot of the hill take the first footpath on the right. Cross the pasture to a ladder stile, and from here follow the obvious path around the north and east shores of the tarn, passing below The How.

At the eastern extremity of the tarn walk up the grassy banking in the direction of a solitary ash tree. At the iron railings find a stile leading into the lane. Turn right here then left at another stile just beyond the ash tree, and trace a path as far as a stony lane (signposted bridleway to Ambleside).

A stiff gradient follows to begin with but soon eases as the way contours around Loughrigg Fell beneath Ivy Crag. Just beyond a TV aerial there is a parting of the way. Ignore the path taking off uphill, and instead keep to the wall side. Windermere now comes into view. About 80 yards beyond a wall corner, take the more obvious right branch when the way divides once again. The bridleway descends for a further half-mile or more through the woods at Miller Brow to reach the

The Way crosses pastureland beside Elterwater on Day 9.
Langdale Pikes can be seen in the distance

Under Loughrigg road a little west of Ambleside. Turn right along the road then shortly after head left over a fine arched bridge spanning the River Rothay. >>

Before the A591 was built, the Under Loughrigg road connecting Ambleside with Rydal at Pelter Bridge was an important highway, frequently travelled by the Wordsworths, especially Dorothy. It was at Pelter Bridge that she wept after parting from William at Low Wood when, accompanied by their brother John, he set off for Yorkshire to visit Mary, his bride-to-be.

Along the Under Loughrigg road are three dwellings connected with the Wordsworths, Fox How, Fox Ghyll and Loughrigg Holme. The Arnold family, including Dr Thomas Arnold and Matthew Arnold, all at various times resided at Fox How, a property intended as a summer-house. William helped Thomas to design and plan the gardens here and Matthew became a good friend and admirer of the poet. At the foot of the hill in Rydal the Arnold family lodged at Spring Cottage in 1831.

Fox Ghyll was first the home of Thomas de Quincey, then of the Luffs, very close friends of the Wordsworth household, the two families not infrequently calling in on one another for a chat or a poetry reading over supper.

Loughrigg Holme, a little further up the Under Loughrigg road, is a house now called Stepping-Stones which in Wordsworth's day was known as Spring Cottage. It has links with several generations of Wordsworths, being the home of Willy, the poet's youngest son, and also of his great-granddaughter, Dorothy. Here, too, Gordon Wordsworth annotated the poet's manuscripts after William's death.

>> Once over the River Rothay turn right and cross Rothay Park, at the far side passing through a gate and into a lane which becomes Vicarage Road after passing the Church of St Mary the Virgin. At the junction with Milloms Park turn right away from the town centre and walk down Compston Road, following this around the bend at the bottom in front of the White Platts Recreation Ground. >>

Like Grasmere, Ambleside has a rush-bearing tradition. This is held on a Saturday in July when a hymn is sung, the lyric composed by Owen Lloyd, a friend of Wordsworth. The Church of St Mary the Virgin was built in 1854 and since then has been referred to as the Wordsworth Chapel. The structure embodies a Wordsworth memorial window at the eastern end of the north aisle, while other windows commemorate Dorothy, Dora and Mary, and incorporate the family motto, '*veritas*' ('truth').

There has been a settlement in Ambleside since the earliest times, the Romans establishing the fort of Galava near the head of the lake, between the Brathay-Rothay confluence and Waterhead. They shipped in building stone up the lake and similarly transported iron ore to the charcoal-fired smelters in the woods hereabouts.

From Norman times Ambleside developed into a prosperous industrial town which thrived on corn, cotton and bobbin-mills. Several fulling-mills also operated to serve local textile businesses. Today the observant visitor may see the remains of at least two mills complete with waterwheels. Where Stock Ghyll bisects the town, the wheel from a former corn-mill can be seen. Another is located adjacent to the unusual Bridge House beside the main road through town.

William's children, John, Willy and Dora, as well as the Coleridge boys, Derwent and Hartley, all attended school here. The oldest parts of Ambleside are centred upon the medley of tiny interconnected lanes, ginnels and dark grey stone cottages near to the Kirkstone road at the northern extremity of the town. On a sunny summer day little yards and alleys such as Tom Fold evoke Wordsworth's description of a 'little rural town' where 'beams of orient light shoot wide and high'. It was here that Benjamin in *The Wagonner* began his journey, starting out from the Salutation Inn bound for Keswick via the Pass of Dunmail.

Without doubt the town's most unusual building, certainly its most photographed, is Bridge House, a 17th-century cottage spanning the beck near the main carpark at the northern end of town. It probably belonged to Ambleside Hall, although according to local tradition it was built by a Scotsman who wished to avoid paying ground rent. In the mid-19th century the Rigg family lived here, bringing up six children, a remarkable feat considering how small the building is. Today it serves as a National Trust information office.

>> Some 30 yards ahead is a crossroads where Church Street turns off to the left. At the north-eastern end of this, on the corner of its junction with Lake Road, stands the Stampers

Restaurant. This occupies the site of Wordsworth's Old Stamp Office. From the Compston Road-Church Street junction go straight across into Kelsick Road with the library on your right and a carpark to the left, to meet yet another junction at the top. Turn right here then left almost immediately, taking you to Old Lake Road leading off uphill at a tangent to the A591.

When the lane forks after about 130 yards take the right branch and head downhill again. Shortly after a carpark is passed, look for the bridleway signposted to Jenkin Crag and Troutbeck which takes off to the left in front of Lane Foot House. The steep way has a metalled surface initially as it passes between walls. After climbing for five minutes or so, take the right branch (signed Jenkin Crag, Skellghyll Woods and Broad Ings) where the way splits.

The way ahead eases, giving good views across Windermere to the Furness Fells. At the turn-off for Broad Ings continue straight forward along a narrow, walled lane which soon enters the National Trust property of Skellghyll Woods before climbing again. Just by the NT sign follow the bridleway to the left, ignoring the continuing footpath. Another bifurcation is soon reached, where the footpath leading left (sign for Jenkin Crag and Troutbeck) is the route to choose.

The rocky trail climbs beside Stencher Beck, crossing this at a small bridge beyond which a choice of two ways wind uphill. They meet again up ahead, then the way levels out alongside a wall through pleasant broadleaf woods towards High Skellghyll Farm. Beyond this, trace the metalled lane downhill, ignoring a footpath off to the right in preference to a bridleway, reached immediately after crossing Hol Beck. This has a blue waymarking arrow and is signposted for Troutbeck.

This track eventually merges with Robin Lane, a walled track which we now follow to the right, contouring around the hillside for about a quarter of a mile. At this point turn right down a stony track. At the bottom turn left on Holbeck Lane, and then right on a leafy bridleway (fingerpost) after 150 yards, tracing this downhill beside a wall into Town Foot.

The continuing route is straight across the road here, but that is tomorrow's story, and so walkers wishing to avail themselves of the youth hostel at High Cross Castle must turn right down the road (Bridge Lane), following this for three-quarters of a mile. The hostel is up a drive on the right reached immediately after High Cross Lodge. Hotel and guest-house accommodation is available in Troutbeck Bridge, a further three-quarters of a mile along the road.

USEFUL INFORMATION

Accommodation: Wide choice of hotel, guest-house and B&B options in Troutbeck Bridge.

Camping: No convenient sites.

Youth Hostel: High Cross Hostel, Bridge Lane, Troutbeck. Tel: (015394) 43543.

Transport: Service No.555 (Lakeslink) linking Windermere, Ambleside, Rydal, Grasmere, Wythburn Church and Keswick. Service No.516 links Ambleside to Dungeon Ghyll (Langdale) via Elterwater. Also linking Kendal and Windermere (Sundays).

Supplies: Choice of shops in Ambleside and Troutbeck Bridge.

Refreshments: Choice of pubs and cafés in Ambleside and Troutbeck Bridge.

Tourist Information: Church Street, Ambleside. Tel: (015394) 32582. Waterhead Pier, Ambleside. Tel: (015394) 32729.

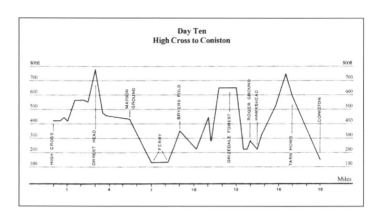

Day Ten
High Cross to Coniston

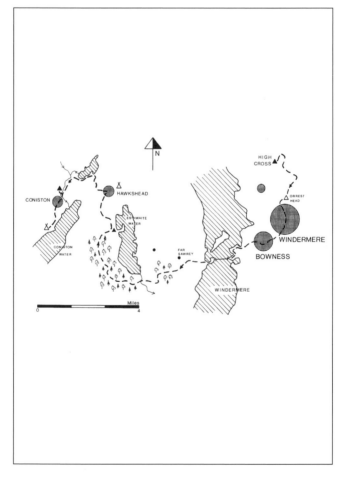

DAY 10
High Cross to Coniston

SUMMARY

Distance: 19 miles (to town centre or Holly How YHA hostel). Add 2.5 miles if starting at High Cross YHA hostel, and in each case add 1.5 miles to Coniston Hall campsite or 4 miles to Crook Farm campsite.

Total Ascent: 1,581 feet (482 metres).

Expected Duration: 7–8 hours (allow an extra 1.5 hours for exploring Hawkshead).

Map: 1:25000 Outdoor Leisure Series sheet Nos.6, 7.

Terrain and Difficulty: This is a long stage mostly through undulating forested country. It is coincident in parts with the Grizedale Forest Sculpture Trail, the Cumbria Way and the Dales Way.

Highlights: Bowness cable ferry, the well-preserved olde-worlde charm of Hawkshead town, Tarn Hows and views of the Furness Fells.

Option: None.

Trout Beck at this point runs in a deep ravine with no way across adjacent to the youth hostel. In order to reach the continuation of the walk, turn left out of the hostel and up Bridge Lane, retracing yesterday's steps to Ford Lane Barn at Town Foot. Turn right immediately before the barn, along a bridleway (fingerpost) which crosses Trout Beck at two foot-bridges then climbs up to join the Kirkstone Pass road (A592).

Turn right along this and after about 230 yards take the first footpath on the left at a kissing gate marked by a finger-post and adjacent to a large Californian redwood. From the gate a vague path gradually rises forward and to the right by a solitary larch tree, over a small brook and around the hillside to reach a stile.

Cross the stile and walk between two farm buildings and forward along a track to a metalled lane a few yards in front. Walk up the lane almost directly opposite (signposted footpath to Far Orrest). Just after Holehird Cottage the track divides, the way straight ahead leading down into a farm. Take the left-hand branch instead, following this to Far Orrest.

Passing the first farmhouse on your right will take you to a junction of footpaths. Ignore the one off to the right (signposted Windermere) and another straight forward (signposted Barburn). Instead turn left over a ladder stile and then sharp right alongside the fence and through a gate into a green lane. Leave this by way of a kissing gate opposite and turn right along the wall and through another gate. Cross the lane here through yet another gate and walk straight forward along the lower edge of a pasture to pick up a ladder stile at the far side.

Cross the stile and turn half left over another stile 100 yards ahead, beyond which you should proceed straight forward along the left edge of the field to cross a step stile at the far left-hand corner. Continue forward in the direction of Near Orrest farmhouse, over a second step stile 50 yards ahead and through a kissing gate. From here follow yellow direction arrows forward around the right-hand side of the farm to enter a metalled lane.

The view of Lake Windermere from Orrest Head

Turn right here and after 200 yards take the first footpath on the left at a step stile (fingerpost). Continue forward beside a wall and go onwards uphill beneath some power lines. The route is vague one moment, obvious the next, but runs parallel and some 50 feet from the wall over to the right. Soon the way negotiates a step stile in the wall, beyond which an obvious path climbs to the magnificent viewpoint at Orrest Head. The view takes in the full extent of Windermere, the Furness Fells in the west, the central fells and Langdale Pikes to the north-west, Morecambe Bay to the south, the Fairfield group and, in the east, the softened skyline of the Howgill Fells.>>

Orrest Head is still a good viewpoint, but because of tree growth the views of the poet's Winandermere (Windermere) are not as extensive as in William's day. There is little that can be said to compliment a town like Windermere, so raped by 'progress' in the name of tourism. When the railway arrived in 1847 it was to transform the town in a way anticipated by William in his sonnet, *Railway*. Until the arrival of the railway, Windermere was a hamlet called Birthwaite, but has expanded today into what passes for an oversized pleasure park, the soonest passed the better.

At over 11 miles in length the lake itself is the largest in England, but only its western shoreline, mostly fringed with woodland, has escaped the level of development which plagues the opposite bank. Heaven knows the catastrophe that would have been unleashed elsewhere had the railway, as originally planned, been extended through Ambleside and, by way of a tunnel beneath Dunmail Raise, onwards to Keswick.

>> The continuing path descends on the south-west side quickly reaching an iron kissing gate. Turn right at this point. The path extends between a fence and wall, very soon reaching a point where a trail takes off left. Ignore this to continue down the wall side through the trees to another parting of the ways. The more obvious route turns left (white waymark arrow on wooden post) but our route is straight forward following the wall to a gate and step stile. Turn left at this point and right into an old walled lane (yellow direction arrows).

Follow the obvious way through rhododendron thickets to a fork. Take the right branch, still tracing the lane to a track crossing right to left at the bottom. Turn left to eventually merge with a metalled lane. A right turn here enters Windermere at the A591. Turn left and walk up the road out of town in the direction of Kendal, passing the train station and Thwaite Lane on your right.

A little way beyond this is Orrest Head Farm where our route, a footpath (fingerpost), takes off to the right. Walk down the side of the cowsheds and head for the field corner where a gate is found. Once through this, walk straight forward to a kissing gate at the far side of the next pasture and beyond, maintaining the same bearing for about 150 yards to reach an iron kissing gate by the railway embankment.

After passing through this gate, bear half left to cross the railway line. Walk between the garages into the housing estate and along Gill Road for about 80 yards, taking a narrow lane leading off to the left by two conifers. Follow this around to the left and straight on at a minor crossroads, the narrowing lane crossing a small stream. Turn right beyond the ford, the narrow lane quickly becoming an open tarmac path beside a housing development. Eventually a gate is reached and a path leads left for School Knott. Go through the gate but ignore the path.

Continue up the lane to a T-junction and turn left along the lane for Matson Ground. Over the wall on the right there are views across to the Furness Fells of Wetherlam, Swirl Howe and Coniston Old Man. After nearly half a mile a pond on the right marks the outskirts of Matson Ground. Turn right at a kissing gate just after the pond to follow the closing stages of the Dales Way long-distance footpath.

From the gate walk downhill beside the fence, cross the farm track and take the well-defined path straight forward (marked with Dales Way discs). The way briefly takes to a metalled track, then crosses rough pastures to a gate in a wall corner. Go through this and bear left, soon to enter a lane that crosses a farm track and continues forward to a gate where Windermere comes into view.

From the gate the way begins its descent towards the lake and Bowness, the uppermost reaches of the latter being entered by Brantfield House. Continue down the hill to the town centre at a crossroads. Walk straight across down St Martins Hill to the church, bearing left in front of this and walking past the Lakeland steamer piers. Turn right soon afterwards into Glebe Road. By the Windermere Quays visitor centre carry on straight forward (footpath signposted Cock-

The descent into Bowness as storm clouds loom over Lake Windermere

shott Point), following a pleasant loop path on the approach to the Bowness ferry landing-stage. There are good views across to Belle Isle with its audacious summer-house.

Upon reaching the public slipway walk straight forward (signposted To the Ferry) and when the road is reached turn right here to the ferry point 150 yards ahead. It is now necessary to take the boat to the far shore, and is a relief indeed to step aboard and escape the commercialised atmosphere of Bowness and nearby Windermere, both startling examples of the bad taste to which Wordsworth referred, and which he feared would result from an influx of tourists.

At the far side landing-stage walk up the road as far as the National Trust carpark at Ash Landing. Here trace a path (signposted Claife Heights and Hawkshead) through tree cover which, after about five minutes' uphill walking, gains The Station, a ruin and vantage-point from which to view the lake. >>

Bowness as a centre is little better than its larger neighbour unless the visitor's interest rests with boats and trinket shops. An exception, perhaps, is the Steamboat Museum, which has on display, amongst other interesting exhibits, the oldest mechanically powered boat in the world, a vessel called *Dolly*, as well as the *Esperance*, which is on record as the oldest boat on Lloyd's Register, and one which featured in Arthur Ransome's classic children's adventure story *Swallows and Amazons* as Captain Flint's houseboat.

Amid the brash trappings of tourism one needs to search deep to find the little morsels of history. For example, opposite the church is a converted school building, known as Wordsworth Court. A foundation stone outside it came from an earlier structure, a school opened by William when he laid the stone in question. The ferry, too, is a quite unusual cable-operated vessel.

Belle Isle, known as Long Holm until renamed in the 19th century, has seen some form of human occupation since Roman times. Ownership of this, the largest island in the lake, passed through several hands, and eventually to the Curwen family who have maintained a summer-house here since 1774. After initially criticising what they considered to be the crass decision to build on Belle Isle, the Wordsworths seem to have eaten humble pie, for when the poet's son, the Reverend John Wordsworth, wed Isabella Curwen in October 1830, they visited the summer-house and grew to appreciate its isolated situation.

>> The continuation up the road from the Ash Landing car-park consists of about half a mile of steep walking. At first on the right-hand side of the road, then continuing on the left, a footpath parallel with the road allows the walker to avoid the traffic. When the road has to be rejoined by the sign for Far Sawrey, continue up the hill to a house on the crest. Immediately beyond this, a footpath (fingerpost) off to the left is followed through a kissing gate then downhill again alongside a wall, heading for a church with Far Sawrey visible across to the right. >>

Beyond the ferry landing the walker enters Beatrix Potter country, where many locations were used in the popular children's stories of Peter Rabbit, Jemima Puddleduck and the like. The Station was a favourite viewpoint in William's time, allowing the observer an expansive panorama of the lake and all its islands. The ruins here are all that remains of Belle View, a building designed for the benefit of visitors who came to admire the panorama. A book used to be kept here so that visitors could record their comments about the vista. The steep hill up from the ferry landing, in particular the point known as Briers Brow, was where William met a discharged soldier while on his way back from Cambridge during the holidays (*The Prelude*, iv.387–425).

>> After the church turn left along the lane at Town End then right almost at once where the cottages finish. Follow the footpath (fingerpost) across a stream and forward to where within a few paces the continuing path takes off at a tangent to the right (yellow arrows), uphill initially but soon levelling out alongside a fence to a stile. Cross this and go forward through a gate to negotiate a second stile. Cross a pasture with wooded hills on either flank to yet a further stile at the far side, and from this point trace a winding trail down through Garnett Wood to a metalled lane after quarter of a mile.

Turn left and, after crossing the Cunsey Beck, turn right along the road. The monotony of these lanes is relieved by the many blossoms of blackthorn, violet, primrose, celandine and anemone. Where the trees come down to the road after a further quarter-mile, turn left on a bridleway for High Dale Park, entering the extensive Graythwaite Woods, part of the Grizedale Forest famous as the place referred to in William's verse, *Nutting*. Within a few yards take the right fork (green direction arrow). The way is mostly obvious but where doubts exist the route is indicated by arrows.

As the way forward levels out, bear right and shortly cross a forestry track to carry on straight forward (arrows), descending now to where the forest ends. Go through a gate here and walk right along a track, following it right then left, downhill to a road. Turn right here and after 150 yards pick up a bridleway winding off uphill on the left through a cleared area. Tough going persists for half a mile as far as a forest access road where a path branches away to the left, guarded by a wooden sculpture of a bat, no less.

Turn right along the track following part of the Grizedale Forest Sculpture Trail, briefly leaving the trees at a gate, before the bridleway, winding to the left, joins another forestry road. Turn right along this for 130 yards to spot height point 203 on the map where a left-hand bend sports another sculpture, this time of a dog. Bear right here and then immediately left, taking a footpath (yellow arrows) diving briefly through conifers to another open area where a gate is reached. Shortly after this the way meets a forestry track at a loop bend.

Follow the left branch forward (yellow arrows) for around 450 yards. Where some power lines intersect the track take the footpath off down to the right. This crosses a replanted area to a gate in a deer fence. Go through this and across a small stream, walking forward a few yards then right along a track to High Barn Farm. The way through the latter is indicated by yellow arrows. Once clear of the buildings bear left along a path extending to the bottom of the pasture and a stile.

Go through the stile and follow the winding path to the bottom of the hill where it bears to the right, crosses a stream and reaches a stile and a gate. Go through this and follow a track beside a ravine to enter a neat little hamlet shortly before meeting the road. Turn left along the road towards Hawkshead and, 180 yards ahead, turn up the access track to Howe Farm, taking off right just by this along the public path for Roger Ground.

At the perimeter of this hamlet go through a gate, cross the stream then bear left up the way to join a lane at a sweeping bend. Bear right here and head downhill for some 60 yards or so to pick up a path on the left (signposted Hawkshead Church). The well-used pathway is flanked by hedges and fenced in places, as are other pastures away to the left, by walls fashioned from thin slabs of stone, a 13th-century technique known as vaccary walls.

Where the church comes into view there is a parting of the ways at a gate. At this point there is a superb view across the town and away to the Helvellyn Range to the north. Turn right for the church but immediately before you reach it veer downhill to the right to find a gate. Go through this, passing Hawkshead Grammar School on your left to meet the road. >>

This school was founded in 1585 by Letters Patent of Elizabeth I, granted at the petition of Edwin Sandys, Archbishop of York, who was born locally. One of the school's principal patrons was Daniel Rawlinson, born at Grizedale near Hawkshead in 1614, and later a one-time vintner in London whose premises were often patronised by Samuel Pepys. The building is interesting in that the red sandstone architraves and mullioned windows were added in 1891 by Lieutenant-Colonel Myles Sandys of Graythwaite Hall, a direct descendant of its founder. Above the door is a curious tablet surmounted by a sundial. The school has been preserved exactly as it was in Wordsworth's day, and still has a desk with his name carved into the wood.

>> Immediately across from the school is the Information Centre and carparks flanking the road leading to the nearby village of Colthouse a quarter of a mile distant, and where for a time William had lodgings. To continue for the town centre, however, turn left along Main Street passing a turning on the left into The Square, and continuing forward with the Queen's Head pub and Beatrix Potter Gallery on your right. Turn left in front of Barclays Bank and head up Vicarage Lane which, at the top, narrows beneath an arch known as Grandy Nook. A few yards beyond the Grandy Nook Teashop can be seen a cottage on the right where, for a short period, Ann Tyson lived before moving to nearby Colthouse. >>

While at school in Hawkshead, William and his brother, Richard, were fortunate to be lodged with Ann Tyson, for she accorded them an uncommon amount of freedom to roam at will throughout the surrounding countryside. William listened to the ice cracking on nearby Esthwaite Water during winter evenings at Ann's Colthouse home. He enjoyed ice skating on the lake, and in summer would set off early to school so that on the way he could stroll around its shoreline, a circuit of some five miles. Wordsworth had some of the happiest moments in his young life after being shipped to school in Hawkshead at Whitsuntide 1779.

Hawkshead is without doubt one of the best-preserved towns in the Lake District. In the 18th century it was a bustling market town thriving on the woollen trade and other local industries such as charcoal-burning and iron ore-smelting. There are many timber-framed buildings dating from the 17th century set in narrow lanes, yards and ginnels.

>> To continue for Coniston, return to the parting of the ways up the hill behind the church and take the other pathway (signposted Tarn Hows, Coniston and Grizedale Forest). From the kissing gate head for the far right-hand corner of the field to enter and follow a lane to Walker Ground.

Where a track is joined at a T-junction turn left (signed Tarn Hows) and after 20 yards go right through a kissing gate. Proceed straight forward for a few paces to a fence, then turn left uphill beside it to reach another kissing gate, at which point there are good views back towards Hawkshead.

The wide path now climbs uphill, crossing countryside in

which Wordsworth hunted woodcocks. Eventually a small stream is crossed to reach a gate with open pastures stretching ahead. The obvious way forward continues straight ahead over a rise, then crosses a farm track, about 160 yards beyond this joining the road outside Hawkshead Hill. Walk through the village to where the road splits. Take the right-hand branch (signposted Tarn Hows), then turn right yet again at the following junction (signposted Ambleside).

Continue along the road for approximately 180 yards then pick up a footpath off to the left up the driveway to Rose How (Tarn Hows Hotel on map). Walk between the buildings up to a gate then go along a narrow, walled lane to a second gate, beyond which the path keeps to the edge of a conifer plantation. Just beyond the next gate a track is intersected crossing from right to left, but continue straight forward and turn right over a stile at a wall corner. Initially the way keeps to the edge of the wood but soon diverges from this to cross a pasture over a rise towards a tiny disused cottage called Rose Castle.

Walk around the cottage and to the left as far as a fingerpost and here turn sharp right downhill to reach a lakeside path. Turn left along this. Tarn Hows is owned by the National Trust and consists of pine and larch woodland with an irregular-shaped tarn near its centre. Tarn Hows was artificially created in the 19th century but today is an established home to breeding and migrating waterfowl, including swans, coots, geese and a variety of ducks.

Just before reaching the outlet from the lake, turn uphill to the left to reach the road by the National Trust carpark, then turn right here to follow the road for almost half a mile. Turn right (signposted public footpath) through a kissing gate and walk along the access track to Tarn Hows Cottage, following this eventually around to the right to reach the front of the cottage. This approach affords good views across into Yewdale.

Go through the first gate facing the house, then bear immediately left through a second gate and a third one a few yards ahead. This pleasant stage descends through woodland, at first alongside a wall and then crossing two deer fences. After this, the path is traced forward through young birch woods which soon thin out alongside Yewdale Beck to a stile. Cross the latter and keep to the fence side on the far right of the pasture, with Yewdale Cottages on the right. Yewdale

Tarn Hows with the Langdale Pikes visible in the distance

Crags tower above and it was here that William pursued the perilous pastime of collecting ravens' eggs.

When a stile is met, cross this and walk forward along a bridleway (signposted Boon Crag, Coniston and Cumbria Way), crossing the bridge from the right. Continue between the hedge and the streambank, here dotted with wood sorrel, anemone, violet and celandine. After about 180 yards the bridleway is left in favour of the Cumbria Way which takes off across a field to the right.

At the far side go through a gate and veer over to the left and forward along a path parallel to a wall enclosing Guards

Wood. Aim for the far left-hand corner of the pasture to briefly enter the woods again before descending through gorse thickets to Shepherd Bridge on the outskirts of Coniston. Coniston Old Man, scarred by quarries and spoil heaps, can be seen overshadowing the village on the right (west).

Walkers staying at the youth hostel (a ten-minute walk away) should cross the bridge and turn right, following the lane to a junction with the A593 Ambleside road. Cross the main road and walk forward up the lane (signposted Youth Hostel Coniston Holly How). The entrance to the hostel is 100 yards up here on the left. Those staying in the village or camping should turn left after crossing Shepherd Bridge. After 200 yards turn right along Tilberthwaite Avenue, passing the Information Centre on the left and on into the village centre at the road junction just beyond St Andrew's Church.

There is a good choice of accommodation in the village, but if you wish to stay at the campsite cross the bridge over Church Beck and walk along the A593 Torver road for about a quarter of a mile. Just beyond the limits of the village pick up a path striking left across the pastures towards the lake shore. Obvious field paths are traced to Coniston Hall. Just before the latter, go through a gate to the left of a barn; then, passing in front of and around to the right of the hall, bear left to enter the Coniston Hall campsite.

Today Coniston, like many centres in Lakeland, depends very much on tourism for its survival, yet its prosperity today is without doubt influenced by its host mountain, Coniston Old Man. The range, which includes Dow Crag, Wetherlam and Swirl How, consists of strata referred to as the Borrowdale Volcanics, capping the underlying slates and shales.

In the 18th century slate was quarried and possibly as early as Norman times people mined copper deep beneath the flanks of the grey mountain. The painter J.M.W. Turner (1775–1851) once stayed at the Black Bull Inn, a former coaching-inn, and the grave of the author, artist and critic John Ruskin (1819–1900) can be found in the grounds of the Anglican church (St Andrews) together with a memorial in the form of a Celtic cross.

Coniston Hall, by the lakeside a little south of the village, is the area's oldest building and once belonging to the Fleming family who later moved to Rydal Hall. The rather gloomy-looking hall has tall, rounded chimneys mentioned by

Wordsworth when referring to the 'neglected mansion house' in his long autobiographical work, *The Prelude*.

Directly across the lake from the campsite, the large white house seen on the distant shore is Brantwood, home for some 29 years to John Ruskin. A museum celebrating the life and work of Ruskin is located in Coniston along the Ambleside road towards the youth hostel.

USEFUL INFORMATION

Accommodation: Choice of hotel, guest-house and B&Bs in Coniston.

Camping: Coniston Hall campsite (one mile south of town). Open Easter to end of October. Full facilities. £3/night/person. Crook Farm campsite, Torver (2.5 miles beyond Coniston Hall). Open all year. Shower and WC. £2/night/person. Also B&B, packed lunches, shop.

Youth Hostels: Esthwaite Lodge, Hawkshead. Tel: (015394) 36293. Holly How hostel, Far End, Coniston. Tel: (015394) 41323. Coppermines House hostel, Coppermines Valley, Coniston. Tel: (015394) 41261.

Transport: Service No.505/506 (Coniston Rambler) links Windermere and Coniston calling at Bowness pier and Hawkshead.

Supplies: Shops, cafés and restaurants in Windermere, Bowness, Hawkshead and Coniston.

Refreshments: Cafés and pubs in Windermere, Bowness, Hawkshead and Coniston. In summer an ice-cream van sells drinks at the National Trust carpark at Tarn Hows.

Tourist Information: Victoria Street, Windermere. Tel: (015394) 46499. Main carpark, Hawkshead. Tel: (015394) 36525. Yewdale Road, Coniston. Tel: (015394) 41533.

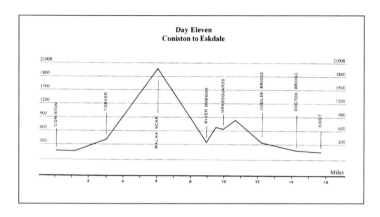

Day Eleven
Coniston to Eskdale

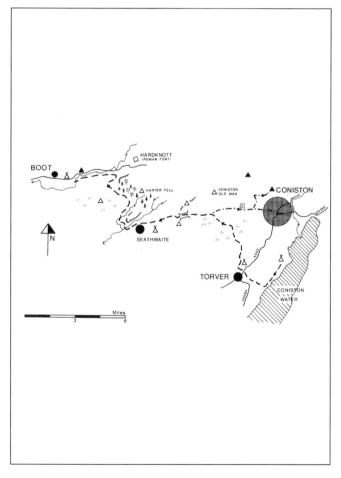

DAY 11
Coniston to Eskdale

SUMMARY

Distance: 12.5 miles (to Holmrook youth hostel starting from Coniston or Holly How hostel) or 15.75 miles (starting at Coniston Hall campsite). In each case add 1.5 miles to Boot village and Hollins Farm campsite.

Total Ascent: 2,723 feet (830 metres).

Expected Duration: 5–7 hours.

Map: 1:25000 Outdoor Leisure Series sheet No.6.

Terrain and Difficulty: Some steep gradients, crosses open fells, followed by woodland and a felled section requiring careful route-finding.

Highlights: Views of Dow Crag, the River Duddon and its tributary, Tarn Beck. The descent into Eskdale.

Option: None.

VILLAGE CENTRE START

Those walkers having stayed in hotels or guest-houses should leave the village centre by crossing the bridge over Church Beck, as if heading for Torver on the A593, and take the very first turning to the right, a lane leading through Dixon Ground. This is signposted to the Sun Hotel, an old coaching-inn that achieved importance when Walna Scar Road was still a principal line of communication into the Duddon Valley.

After 150 yards, walk in front of the inn and follow the lane left slightly, then around bends first to the right and then to the left again, to reach a complex junction. The way leads straight forward up a very steep continuation beneath trees for a little less than quarter of a mile. The gradient from here then levels out for a further half-mile to a gate and carpark that mark the end of the metalled section. To continue from here, follow directions as described for the Youth Hostel Start below.

YOUTH HOSTEL START

If departing from the youth hostel turn left out of the driveway and walk up the hill slightly towards some cottages. A left turn here (fingerpost) takes you to a public footpath up a stony

Walkers on the Walna Scar 'road' between Coniston and the Duddon Valley

track to a gate within a few yards. Go through this and turn left alongside a wall, tracing a footpath contouring towards woods at Holywath. Here the path merges with an old mining road leading to the Coppermines Valley.

Walk uphill for approximately quarter of a mile, the path soon running parallel to a deep, wooded ravine. At the top end of this is Miner's Bridge. To reach the youth hostel at Coppermines House, go on up the track, but to continue the walk turn left through a gate, cross the bridge and, ignoring the obvious path left down the far side of the ravine, walk forward and left around the end of a wall.

Continue along a path contouring and then gradually climbing around a shoulder giving fine views up the Coppermines Valley to Swirl How and across Coniston. The path soon levels briefly before becoming a switchback trail alongside a wall and down to a footbridge across Scrow Beck. Cross this to a gate then walk uphill with a wall on your left to reach a second gate on top of the rise. Through this, continue along the wall, following this to a stile where Walna Scar Road is met. Turn right up the road and continue to the carpark at the end of the metalled road after half a mile.

Go through the gate here and proceed forward along the obvious bridleway, a broad track heading up the fellside. The bridleway crosses a quaint packhorse bridge where the rock architecture of Dow Crag can be seen over to the right. The cliffs here are famous for their earlier association with pioneer rock-climbing in England.

When the top of the pass is finally gained, a whole new panorama opens in front, stretching across the Duddon Valley towards the trident-like summit of Harter Fell in the middle distance. Away to the right of this the skyline formed by the central fells is dominated by the high Scafells. The distant horizon to the left of Harter Fell is punctuated by the upright profile of the Sellafield Nuclear Reprocessing Plant. From the top of the pass follow instructions for Main Route Continuation.

CAMPSITE START

From Coniston Hall campsite walk along the track through the camping park to its southernmost extremity, following yellow direction arrows to the left of a small copse to locate a kissing gate by the water's edge. Beyond this the path continues along the lakeside to the far end of the next pasture. Cross a step stile and footbridge and trace the shoreline path (marked Cumbria Way in places), passing the Hoathwaite Landing to enter the woodlands of Torver Common. >>

Coniston Water is a much more placid lake than Winder-mere and was originally called Thurston's Mere. It has three small islands, one of which, known as Wild Cat Island, featured in Arthur Ransome's story *Swallows and Amazons*.

Coniston Water has seen both the slowest and fastest methods of water transport. The steam yacht *Gondola*, first launched in 1859, was recovered from the lake bed in 1977, restored by the National Trust, and today provides passenger services on the lake in summer. It looks like a cross between a steam yacht and the craft that ply the canals of Venice. At the opposite extreme, Coniston Water has since 1939 been the site of several water speed record bids, when Malcolm Campbell in the very first *Bluebird* established a new world record of 141.74mph. This association with speed ended tragically when Donald Campbell (1921–67), in his endeavours to push his own record to over 300mph, was killed when his *Bluebird* somersaulted and crashed on 4 January 1967. He had reached an estimated speed of 320mph.

>> After passing a wall and crossing a brook adjacent to the Coniston launch jetty, a clearing is entered where our route branches off to the right, uphill, heading for Torver. In less than a quarter of a mile from the clearing, a track branches off right across a stream. Ignore this and continue forward along the more obvious way, passing through young mixed deciduous forest. A track is met coming from the left. Follow this beside a wall to reach a gate.

Beyond the gate, easy walking for Brackenbarrow Farm gives fine views over to the right, of Coniston Old Man and Wetherlam. After passing some ruined barns the way narrows between mossy walls and can be overgrown with brambles. At the farm cross the stile and turn left along a track, in a short while crossing a minor road and tracing a footpath downhill towards a ruined wall. Beyond this cross a disused railway and trace a fence line and wall to the road by Brig House.

Turn left over the bridge and take the first turning right (signposted Coniston Old Man and Walna Scar). Walk uphill, after a few yards bearing left where the lane forks (signed Walna Scar, Crook Farm, camping/B&B). Within a few yards a T-junction is met where Crook Farm campsite is to the right. Our continuing route, however, bears left, around a sweeping corner and uphill, eventually following a stony bridleway, a narrow, walled lane ascending towards the open moor.

After rounding a corner by an abandoned quarry, the route then lies straight forward up the hillside by further old quarries. Walna Scar Road can be seen snaking up the flanks of Coniston's Old Man and over the shoulder of Brown Pike. Eventually a stream is crossed by a climbing hut, formerly a gunpowder magazine, and the way shortly reaches a gate, where the bridleway (look for blue direction arrows) bears right through two gates, over a stream, and winds its way through slate quarry spoil heaps.

Beyond these, pass a flooded quarry into which plunges a powerful waterfall. The way skirts around the right-hand (north-west) side of this pit, and after about a further quarter-mile of climbing meets Walna Scar Road ascending from the right. Turn left along this and continue the climb. The going is steep but rest-stops are graced with views back over Coniston Water and away beyond to Morecambe Bay.

Walna Scar Road was often walked by Wordsworth, particularly while he was at school in Hawkshead, on his fishing trips to the Duddon Valley, or on horseback expeditions to the Duddon Sands and Furness Abbey.

MAIN ROUTE CONTINUATION

The valley into which our route now begins its descent is one of my personal favourites, a magnificent corner of the Lake District, quieter than other dales and endowed with many Wordsworthian associations. From the top of the pass the bridleway traverses south-west across the flank of White Pike, then north-west tracing the boisterous course of Long House Gill more or less all the way into the valley. Across this can be seen the gash of Wallowbarrow Gorge and in front of this the knobbly ridgeline of The Pen, a name surviving from Celtic times.

When a metalled lane is met by a bridge, continue along it and forward through a gate, shortly after a cottage taking a path through another gate on the left (fingerpost). Bear half left from here towards a power-line pole, following the transmission lines to High Moss Centre, passing this on its right and tracing a track across meadows to Turner Hall Farm. Just before reaching this the way veers right over a small stream, then left to a gate. Continue beyond this, down a metalled lane to its junction with the valley road, and turn left.

Walk down the road towards Seathwaite, or use the parallel pathways in the woods on the right, a much easier option for tired feet. Soon Tarn Beck is heard, then its foaming course glimpsed between the trees. Several points along its tumultuous banks offer choice places to stop for lunch or a breather to contemplate the *14th Duddon Sonnet* in which the stream is described. The walker is urged, however, to be patient until reaching the woods beside the River Duddon, an idyllic nook where the poet's presence may be sensed even more strongly.

When the Church of the Holy Trinity is reached at Seathwaite, turn right on a public footpath (fingerpost) and with difficulty negotiate a very narrow gap stile. Ignore the path following the riverbank to the right, and instead proceed straight forward across two fields and turn left for the Newfield Inn. >>

The Church of the Holy Trinity at Seathwaite replaced an earlier structure in 1874. The previous building was the subject of a sonnet by Wordsworth. When it was later under threat of demolition, Ruskin tried to save it. There is more than one set of stepping-stones crossing the Duddon, but the ones over the river near Seathwaite without doubt best fit the verse.

>> From the inn continue down the road for 100 yards then take off right through a gate on a path signposted to Wallowbarrow. Cross the footbridge over the beck and follow the stream left as far as its confluence with the larger Duddon. Climb the wooded banking and in a few minutes alight upon a picturesque set of hippings (stepping-stones). >>

It would, I'm sure, be difficult to imagine a more charming setting, which is all the more alluring for its vernal simplicity. The woods on both sides of the river are noted for their many impressive anthills, and in summer are carpeted with bluebells. This juxtaposition of sparkling river, woodland and wild blooms evokes some of the lines in *Tables Turned* and *Wordsworth's Immortality Ode* (i.1–9).

The series of 34 sonnets about the River Duddon were published in 1820 to widespread acclaim. These covered the birth of the river near the Three Shires Stone on Wrynose Pass, to its outfall in the Duddon estuary. It was this of all rivers that held a special place in the poet's heart: it was down the Duddon that he had often travelled on fishing expeditions while still at school in Hawkshead, and which he warmly

Crossing the River Duddon stepping-stones at Seathwaite on Day 11

recalled from a time spent along its banks with his wife Mary on their way back from the coast.

>> The route continues on the far bank of the Duddon. If the river is in spate walk upstream from the stepping-stones to find and cross a footbridge. Follow a well-worn footpath west from the riverbank to a gate, and through this proceed towards High Wallowbarrow Farm. Negotiate two gates into the farmyard, where a right turn (bridleway to Grassguards) out of the farm climbs the hill through birch woods flanking Wallowbarrow Crag. The ascent is relentless for the first half-mile, but in summer entertainment can often be found in

admiring rock gymnasts perform on the adjacent cliffs, or watching for peregrine falcon, a rare raptor now nesting at this site.

Beyond Low Crag the gradient eases and the continuing bridleway passes beneath Basin Barrow with Harter Fell soaring out of the forest ahead. Over to the right, across the Duddon, our earlier route down Walna Scar can be seen snaking down across the Seathwaite Fells. Before too long the route ahead descends across a fertile area of pastureland to the farm at Grassguards. Pass through the farmyard and turn left just before the watersplash, ignoring a footbridge in favour of a stile. Cross this and walk beside the wall to a gate.

Once beyond the gate cross a forest track, through a second gate and proceed forward into the forest. Within a few strides cross to the far stream bank (indicated by blue arrows), then turn left. An obvious path climbs up through the clearing following Grassguards Gill. A little over half a mile from the farm a parting of the ways marked on the map is not clear on the ground, but after passing a small cairn a fingerpost is soon reached which indicates the way over to the right through a gate providing entry through a non-existent fence.

The bridleway now sneaks through the low point between Ulpha and Harter Fells. To begin with, however, it crosses a scene of utter desolation where the forest has been felled and replanted on the flanks of Harter Fell. In places the way is indistinct and confused by fallen timber and brashings, and one must search carefully for the marker posts bearing blue arrows. About 100 yards beyond the fingerpost a bridleway is met going from left to right, back into the forest. Turn left along this and eventually meet a gate where the watershed is crossed and the devastation left behind.

The way now begins its descent into Eskdale. After rounding the shoulder of Birker Fell, the walker is greeted by a dramatic panorama, the highest mountains in England forming a backcloth to one of the most delightful dales in the district, a verdant valley that raises its windswept head among the knot of fells representing the highest ground in England, yet dips its feet into the warming shallows of the Irish Sea.

When a broken-down wall is reached with a stream beyond it, the bridleway veers away half right to contour along the hillside, before levelling out towards the valley floor in the direction of Jubilee Bridge at the foot of the Hardknott Pass

Looking across Eskdale towards (from left to right) Scafell, Scafell Pike, Ill Crag, Esk Pike and Bow Fell

hairpins. The remains of the Roman fort (Mediobogdum) are situated above the second bend in the road some 15 minutes' walk from the bridge. Just before the latter, leave the bridle-way and take off sharp left on a footpath beside the wall, following this slightly uphill to reach a kissing gate within a quarter of a mile. >>

The fort at Hardknott was built in *c.*AD130 and is remarkably well preserved, with perimeter walls, angle towers and some buildings surviving several courses high. It was one of several such structures erected by the occupying Romans to protect their military highway extending from Brocavum (Brougham) via Galava (Ambleside) to their west-coast port at Glannaventa (Ravenglass).

>> From the kissing gate a wood is entered just after crossing a stream and then two stiles and a further gate are negotiated. Cross a footbridge and follow what is now a bridleway once more as far as a fingerpost by a parting of the ways a few minutes later. Continue forward (signposted Penny Hill) and cross a stream, almost immediately followed by a gate. Go through this and trace the path beside a wall before

it merges with a farm track. Follow this across the next pasture, through a gate hole and on for Penny Hill Farm. A walled lane passes through the farm and along a track leading to Doctor Bridge.

Walkers heading for the youth hostel should cross the bridge over the Esk and follow the footpath to the right to reach the valley road after 250 yards. Turn right again, passing the Woolpack Inn, to reach the hostel on the left after a quarter of a mile.

Campers must turn left after crossing Doctor Bridge and follow a pleasant riverside trail good for spotting dippers, wagtails and other river-loving birds. After emerging from a short narrow section of walled lane, the way takes a course parallel with the right-hand wall, through gorse bushes, to reach a gate. Beyond this the route contours along the crest of a banking overlooking the Esk, passes through a kissing gate and continues with an impressive array of crags forming the left-hand skyline across the river.

Eventually the bridleway merges with a well-made gravel path, which is followed for a few hundred yards to where a lane turns right at St Catherine's Church. Walk along this for a little less than half a mile, passing Church House and before long meeting the valley road at a crossroads by the Brook House Inn. Hollins Farm campsite is quarter of a mile up the valley road, while Boot village and the continuation of the walk, to Wasdale, lies straight forward from the junction.

USEFUL INFORMATION

Accommodation: B&B at the Woolpack, Brook House and Burnmoor Inns, Boot.

Camping: Hollins Farm, Boot. Open all year. £2/night/person. Showers and WC. Tel: (014967) 23253.

Youth Hostel: Holmrook hostel. Tel: (019467) 23219.

Transport: Lakeland Pick-and-Drop service. Tel: (016973) 44275/42768.

Supplies: Village shop in Boot.

Refreshments: Newfield Inn, Seathwaite. Café at Dalegarth station, Boot. Burnside Inn and Brook House Inn, also in Boot.

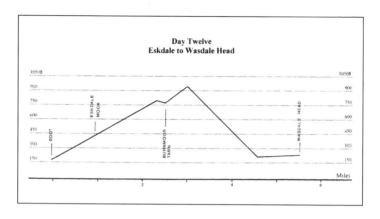

Day Twelve
Eskdale to Wasdale Head

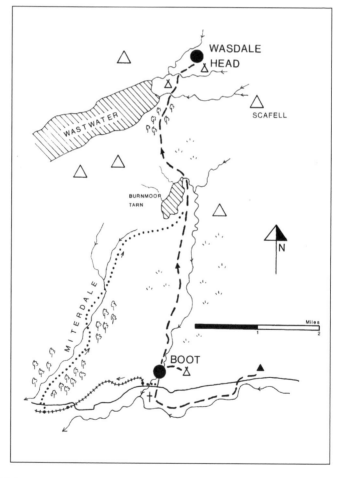

DAY 12
Eskdale to Wasdale Head

SUMMARY

Distance: 5.5 miles (add 2 miles if starting from Holmrook YHA hostel).

Total Ascent: 820 feet (250 metres).

Expected Duration: 2 hours. Add extra 1–2 hours for Miterdale option.

Map: 1:25000 Outdoor Leisure Series sheet No.6.

Terrain and Difficulty: A mostly well-defined bridleway (cairned in places) is traced with minimal difficulties across exposed moorland.

Highlights: Dramatic entry in Wasdale, England's finest valley head, with excellent mountain views.

Option: Narrow-gauge railway and Miterdale.

Walkers starting from the youth hostel should follow Day 11's directions for Boot and from there as below.

Boot is left behind by crossing over the arched bridge beside the old cornmill and climbing up to a gate. Go through this and after 50 yards take the bridleway going through a second gate, this time on the right. From there trace the obvious pony track heading for the open fell, more or less parallel with a wooded gill, Willan Beck. The climbing is steep to begin with but eventually levels out onto Eskdale Moor.

After some time a gate is reached by a wall corner. Ignore the track rising uphill to the left just before this, and instead slip through the gate to continue forward along a track, less distinct at first, but heading towards a building seen in the distance, with the craggy Eskdale Fell rising over to the right.

Easy, level going continues across Eskdale Moor, but approximately half a mile before Burnmoor Tarn is reached the route splits at a point marked by a cairn. Take the right-hand fork, a route that eventually makes its way towards the north-eastern shoreline of the tarn where the footpath is met coming from Miterdale.

Beyond Bulatt Bridge a vague trail splits off half right heading for Scafell, but our route veers away left around the end of the lake (look for cairns) and, after about a quarter of a mile, picks its way up a bracken-covered rise. Where a broken, walled enclosure is met the bridleway bears right and climbs to the watershed, levelling out towards the rim of Wasdale. At the far side of the valley Yewbarrow and Kirk Fell stand sentinel at the mouth of Mosedale where tomorrow's continuing route eventually lies. >>

Archaeological evidence suggests that around Burnmoor there was once dense forest with Bronze Age settlements, probably occupying clearings in the tree cover. The first recorded ascent of Scafell Pike, loftiest peak in England, was that made by Samuel Taylor Coleridge in 1802. Some 16 years afterwards, Dorothy Wordsworth climbed the mountain with her close friend Miss Mary Barker.

To say the entry into Wasdale is dramatic would be to understate one of the finest points of this stage of the walk. Some of the best-known mountains of Lakeland form a backcloth to a verdant valley floor that consists of a seemingly random, patchwork-quilt arrangement of walled enclosures. Wastwater itself is the deepest lake in England, sounded to a depth of around two hundred feet, and the view of the valley head from its shores, backed by Great Gable, was adopted as a logo by the Lake District National Park.

>> The stony track soon loses height through Fence Wood, passing the Fell and Rock climbing hut at Brackenclose to meet Lingmell Gill. Turn left down the side of this, cross the bridge to the right and proceed straight ahead passing the large and orderly National Trust campsite partially concealed by trees on the left.

Those wishing to camp at Wasdale Head instead, or take advantage of the hotel or B&B accommodation here, must continue past the National Trust campsite to reach a gate. Go through this and bear half right along the true left bank of the normally dry riverbank for about 60 yards to where a wooden marker post indicates bridleways straight forward and left, directly across the river.

If the latter is in flood, Wasdale Head can only be reached by walking up the valley road from the National Trust camp-site. Otherwise, cross to the far bank and turn immediately right to a gate. Ignore this to follow the footpath traced between a fence and the riverbank, passing through gorse thickets and another gate. After this a wide track between gorse bushes is followed to a kissing gate. Cross a couple of small brooks before eventually meeting the valley road, turning right here into the hamlet. The campsite is in the small paddock over the wall on the right, almost immediately opposite the Wasdale Head Inn.

The bridleway route out of Boot over Burnmoor to Wasdale, and from there over the high Blacksail Pass, was originally a corpse road along which the deceased were carried on horseback from the unconsecrated ground of Ennerdale and Wasdale to the Church of St Catherine in Boot. Tales are legion of horses bolting in fright and being found some time afterwards minus the corpse, or of the dearly departed mysteriously coming back to life in transit! Burnmoor is a wild spot when the weather is less than kind, but in Bronze Age times the climate must have been milder for there is evidence here of settlements dating from around 1800BC.

After being nameless for centuries, the tiny church at Wasdale Head was dedicated to St Olaf as late as 1977. It is among the smallest in the country. A tradition once said that Wasdale Head had the tallest mountain, the smallest church, the deepest lake and the greatest liar in the country! (The latter was Wil Ritson, a former keeper of the inn.) At once moved by the situation, Wordsworth referred to St Olaf's as 'a temple raised by God's own hand'.

MITERDALE OPTION

The narrow-gauge railway may be used for a variation of the route to Wasdale. From Dalegarth station in Boot take the short railway journey down valley and alight at Irton Road. Walk out of the station down a dirt track to the junction with the valley road. Turn left here. Then, around the first bend, take the first right (though lacking a signpost, this is a public bridleway) up a lane. Follow this for three-quarters of a mile, ignoring all turn-offs on either side. This lane is especially rich in flowers, notably herb Bennet, foxglove, stitchwort and bluebell. >>

The Eskdale-to-Ravenglass line, affectionately referred to as the 'La'al Ratty', is England's oldest narrow-gauge railway, the present 15-inch gauge plying the seven miles between Ravenglass and Boot. The railway was built originally as a three-foot

The 'La'al Ratty' narrow-gauge railway can be used for the Miterdale option on Day 12

industrial-gauge line to serve the quarries and mines of the valley, transporting iron ore and stone to the mainline up the west coast.

>> Just before a bridge the way forward opens out into the Miterdale Forest Enterprise land. After crossing the bridge, follow the bridleway winding up to the right towards a wall, and continue along this, occasionally flanked by walls, up a quiet valley where the walker can escape the crowds normally associated with the Lake District. Half a mile from the bridge the path enters Low Place Farm, where a right turn (sign-

posted bridleway for Wasdale) meets a ford over the Miter.

Walk left for a few yards up the true right bank to find a bridge. The river here flows through bright yellow gorse thickets. Cross over and turn left along a stony track for almost half a mile, whereupon a branch veers left to another ford at the Bakerstead Outdoor Pursuits Centre. Ignore this to continue forward beside the wall, beneath the trees. The way climbs between a broken wall and a fence to reach more open country at a stile. The forward view up to this point is dominated by the lofty profile of Scafell.

The going underfoot can be quite boggy along this stage, but as a consequence there are numerous examples of the butterwort, a fly-eating plant commonly found on poorly drained ground. Other typical flowers are milkwort and tormental. The forest ends at a ladder stile, after which the Miter has shrunk to become little more than a mite.

Still following the diminutive river, the path passes through a narrowing of the valley where it squeezes between Tongue Moor and Eskdale Moor. After emerging from this restriction the path diverges from the stream, contours along the slopes of Eskdale Moor and strikes across towards Burnmoor Lodge. Here the way passes to the right of the building, then, on the eastern side of Burnmoor Tarn, joins the bridleway from the right, coming from Boot. To continue from this point follow directions as for the normal route departure from Boot.

USEFUL INFORMATION

Accommodation: B&B at Wasdale Head Inn and Burnthwaite House.

Camping: National Trust campsite at the head of the lake. Open all year. Fee £3/night/person. Full facilities but very regimented. Wasdale Head campsite is smaller and cheaper (£1.50/night/person). Pay at Barn Door Shop. There are WCs beside the inn.

Youth Hostel: Black Sail Hut at the head of Ennerdale is a two-hour walk beyond Wasdale Head. It is essential to book and check opening times in advance. See appendix for address of YHA.

Transport: Lakeland Pick-and-Drop service. Tel: (016973) 44275/42768.

Supplies: Barn Door Shop (open 0900–1730), Wasdale Head.

Refreshments: Wasdale Head Inn.

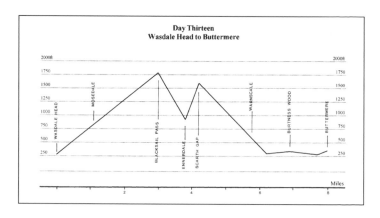

Day Thirteen
Wasdale Head to Buttermere

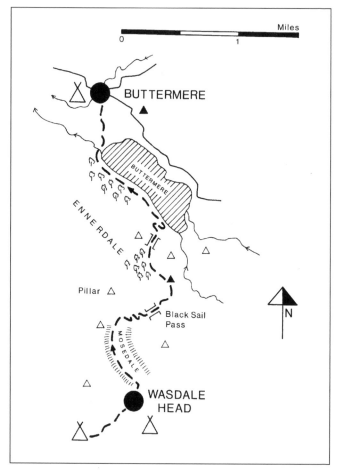

THE WILLIAM WORDSWORTH WAY

DAY 13
Wasdale Head to Buttermere

SUMMARY
Distance: 8 miles.
Total Ascent: 2,165 feet (660 metres).
Expected Duration: 3–4 hours.
Map: 1:25000 Outdoor Leisure Series sheet Nos.4, 6.
Terrain and Difficulty: The route over Black Sail Pass is one of the toughest climbs of the whole walk. The paths are well defined, though some difficulty may be experienced in mist on the descent to Black Sail youth hostel.
Highlights: A dramatic route through superb mountain scenery, taking in the headwaters of the River Liza in upper Ennerdale.
Option: None.

Though perhaps saddened to be leaving behind such superb scenery as that at Wasdale Head, the drama of Mosedale and the Black Sail Pass provides ample compensation. The top of the pass can be reached in under two hours, following a path that winds its serpentine way up out of Mosedale and then, like a striking snake, hurls itself over the pass into the head of Ennerdale.

Starting out from the shop the continuing path, again part of the old corpse way, is gained by walking down the right-hand side of the inn and turning sharp right towards a gate by a neat packhorse bridge. Pass through the gate but do not cross the bridge. Instead, continue forward parallel to the stream, gradually climbing up to the left to reach a gate. Away over to the right can be seen Great Gable (Gavel in Words-worth's time), the steep flanks of Kirk Fell rearing up immediately in front of your nose.

Where the track bears left towards the gate, ignore the path descending to the right towards a stream. With the gate left behind and the path initially hemmed in by walls, the way soon levels out before descending slightly into the fine tributary valley of Mosedale, a mixture of pastel shades forming pleasing contrasts. Across the dale Yewbarrow, one of the steepest hills in the Lakes, is seen almost end on. The so-called Crab's Claw rock formation is visible on its craggy right-hand skyline.

After a little less than a mile, ignore a path that branches off to the right, and follow instead the obvious bridleway as it climbs to a gate in the last of the dry-stone walls. This point marks the beginning of the real hard work in gaining Black Sale Pass, and soon the route is zigzagging up the steep slopes of Gatherstone Head. At last the summit is reached at a cairn.

Leaving Black Sail Pass, a stony path, punctuated by cairns in places, slips steeply down through rock outcrops and scree into the head of Ennerdale, the superbly located youth hostel quickly coming into sight. Away to the left of this secluded refuge, Scarth Gap, the obvious break in the ridge separating High Crag and Haystacks, offers a glimpse, as if through a window, of Whiteless Pike and the hills of the Grasmoor Range. This is but a preview of the magnificent vista to be enjoyed upon passing through the Gap itself.

Near the foot of the descent the bridleway skirts the uppermost edge of the forest that has despoiled this remote dale. A footbridge over the River Liza leads onto a switchback continuation of the path leading as far as the Black Sail hostel, a converted shepherd's bothy. One variant of Wainwright's Coast to Coast Walk passes this way, a higher-level option crossing our route at Scarth Gap. From the front door of this hostel this col is about a half-hour's walk away, the way being a vehicle track as far as the forest gate, then a steeply rising footpath bearing right, up the perimeter of the forest for half a mile. Given clear conditions, Scarth Gap offers views back to Pillar Rock, the magnificent feature from which its host mountain is named. >>

The trees in upper Ennerdale were among the much despised first plantings of the Forestry Commission way back in the 1930s. A peculiar feature worth noting during the descent from Black Sail is the preponderance of rounded, cone-like mounds scattered along the lower flanks of Haystacks, and forming a part of the long spur of Green Gable, known as the Tongue. These moraine deposits are similar in nature to drumlins, and were left behind by retreating glaciers during the last Ice Age, and were subsequently modified by post-glacial weathering.

Pillar Rock is mentioned in *The Brothers*, a poem inspired by the tale of a fatal accident involving a local shepherd who fell from the Rock, an event Wordsworth heard about during his 1799 walking tour of the Lake District with Coleridge.

>> From the wide col of Scarth Gap the Buttermere lake seems hemmed in by high mountains, an impression strengthened by the narrowness of the dale, in which the village and a few hamlets appear as scattered islets in a placid green sea. A route is cairned down through scree slopes contouring across the flanks of Buttermere Fell, the descent towards the lake being rocky and, in places, steep. Away to the right, across the great hollow comprising Warnscale Bottom, the shapely summit of Fleetwith Pike rises like an equilateral pyramid, presiding over the southern flank of the Honister Pass, the motor route over from Borrowdale. >>

Buttermere is the name of a valley, a lake and a tiny village consisting of two hotels, a few farmhouses and a tiny church dedicated to St James and of no great vintage, though it probably stands on the site of an earlier chapel. This is one of the most picturesque valleys in the Lake District, and there is no finer place from which to judge this than the point where

Fleetwith Pike (to the left) and Haystacks seen from the Buttermere campsite

the walk tops Scarth Gap after the climb from Black Sail in Ennerdale. Seen from here, the interplay of colours created by the verdant grass, the bracken and living rock is both satisfying to the eye and beyond compare.

>> A parting of the ways is reached by the corner of a small wood, a sharp right down the far side of this heading towards a gate and footbridge, our route straight ahead taking off downhill towards Buttermere. At the foot of the incline bear left along a bridleway beside the lake.

The way soon crosses a footbridge over Comb Beck, beyond which the way divides. The bridleway takes a rising line left and a permissive path keeps mostly to the lake shore. Both routes enter the National Trust property of Burtness Wood and converge again at the outfall of the lake one mile later. Either way, the pleasant trail winds through open pine woods abounding with flowers and birdlife.

Just before the end of the lake the two routes rejoin, and a few yards beyond this junction a footpath departs left, uphill, signposted to Red Pike. Go through a gate a few yards beyond this, cross two footbridges and some 80 yards further take a left turn through a kissing gate and along a track for a further quarter-mile. The waterfall cascading down between the two bridges is Sourmilk Gill, an impressive spectacle following prolonged rainfall. Where the track turns sharp left a bridleway from Scale Bridge and Scale Force joins from the left. Go through the kissing gate and, a few yards further, bear right in front of the Fish Hotel into the centre of the hamlet.

Beyond the Fish, pass the Croft House Café on the right and Bridge Hotel on the left at the T-junction. The youth hostel is reached by turning right at the junction and following the road left and slightly uphill to a junction by the tiny church. The hostel is a five-minute walk up the valley road from the Newlands Pass turn-off. Cragg Farm (B&B and bunkhouse) is a five-minute walk left down the valley road from the junction at the Bridge Hotel.

The pretty village of Buttermere, nestling in the alluvial ground separating Buttermere from Crummock Water, achieved national recognition in 1802 when the sad story of a young girl won the hearts of the nation. Mary Robinson, the daughter of the innkeeper at the Fish Inn (now a much enlarged hotel), and known locally as the Beauty of Buttermere, had been wed in 1802 to a bigamist by the name of

Hatfield. After masquerading as the Honourable Alexander Hope MP and lavishing high living on his young bride, he was eventually exposed and hanged as a confidence fraudster who had left in his wake fatherless children and broken hearts the length and breadth of the country. William wove this story into his great work, *The Prelude*.

USEFUL INFORMATION

Accommodation: B&B at Cragg Farm, Fish Hotel or Bridge Hotel, Buttermere.

Camping: Syke Farm, Buttermere. Open all year. Fee £3/night/person. Showers, toilets. Tel: (017687) 70222.

Bunkbarn: Cragg Farm Bunkhouse. Open all year. Fee £3/night/person.

Youth Hostel: King George IV Memorial Hostel. Tel: (017687) 70245.

Transport: Service Nos. 77, 77A links Keswick with Buttermere via Grange Bridge, Seatoller, Honister YHA, Lorton and Whinlatter.

Supplies: Café in Buttermere.

Refreshments: Bars in the Bridge and Fish Hotels.

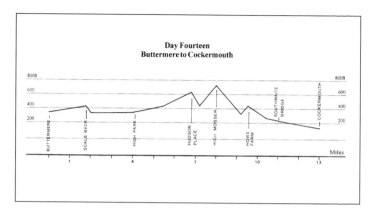

Day Fourteen
Buttermere to Cockermouth

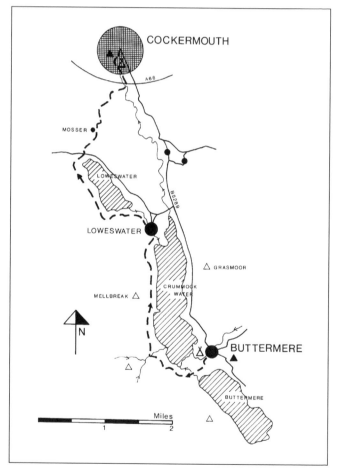

THE WILLIAM WORDSWORTH WAY

DAY 14
Buttermere to Cockermouth

SUMMARY

Distance: 13 miles.

Total Ascent: 797 feet (243 metres).

Expected Duration: 6 hours.

Map: 1:25000 Outdoor Leisure Series sheet No.4.

Terrain and Difficulties: A long stage, mostly utilising field-paths and bridleways. The first half takes in picturesque woodland and lakeside trails, followed by rolling farmland with the occasional hamlet and quiet, metalled lane.

Highlights: Excellent views of the Grasmoor range, back up valley towards Buttermere, and of Scotland, seen across the Solway.

Option: None.

Leave Buttermere village by retracing the previous day's steps passing the Fish Hotel, turning left then right through a kissing gate at the start of the bridleway leading to Scale Bridge and Force. Continue down a narrow lane between a hedge and fence with a hill called Dodd rising immediately ahead and, peering over the ridge to the left of it, the summit of High Stile (2,647 feet). The hedges here are a mass of blackthorn bloom in spring.

Cross the bridge and turn right along a trail beneath mixed deciduous woods where the great spotted woodpecker can often be heard. Away to the right Whiteless Pike is prominent, and to the left of this can be seen the long whaleback ridge of the Grasmoor range through which, two weeks ago, the first day of the walk threaded its tentative way.

Near the start of Crummock Water a cairn marks a parting of the ways, our route bearing to the right, passing a small walled enclosure and continuing parallel to the lake. The flat-topped hill rising immediately in front is Mellbreak, considered by some to be the finest hill in the western Lakes. The way now picks its way through and among a scattering of hawthorn, holly and ash; then, about three-quarters of a mile from Scale Bridge, it veers left away from the lake to become less distinct.

Aim for a point corresponding with the far left extremity of a wooded gill and cross this at the base of a bracken-covered banking. The way on is a green swathe cut through bracken leading towards a gap in a wall. Go through this, cross Scale Beck and turn right down the true left bank of the stream. After a quarter of a mile turn left again along a pleasant lakeside path. (If Scale Beck is in flood and unsafe to cross, there is a footbridge 250 yards downstream of the ford.)

The path beside the lake passes a curious peninsula called Low Ling Crag and then continues for approximately half a mile, at which point a derelict wall is crossed. Some 100 yards beyond this the continuing route takes a vague line uphill to the left, joining a higher terrace path beneath Dropping Crag. Continue uphill over a rise to reach a wall by a gate. Walk forward with the wall on the right, downhill though an oak wood, enjoying distant views down Lorton Vale.

Continue above High Park Farm to a gate, beyond which the walk takes to a leafy, walled path, tracing this forward past Garth Cottage and left along the metalled lane at the end. Cross over the bridge and take the next left for Loweswater village. For the quarter-mile into the village the monotony of the lane is relieved by a profusion of wild blooms, stitchwort, primrose, haw, celandine, blackthorn, wood sorrel and violet being prevalent.

Walk through the village with the church on the right, then turn left at the next junction, continuing up the road past the turning for Thackthwaite. Take the next left, a tarmac lane marked public bridleway and, walking downhill to a fork, bear right through a gate passing the National Trust carpark.

A track is now traced across pastureland towards Loweswater and Watergate Farm. Just before this the way swings away right to a gate and from here enters Holme Wood, consisting of mixed woodland that is an excellent habitat for birdlife and flora. Initially the path keeps to the lakeside, but just beyond a footbridge the way splits, the right branch leading to a shed while our way continues straight on, ignoring other ways taking off left near a ford and a bridge.

After three-quarters of a mile the path leaves the woods behind at a gate, beyond which it rises steadily for Hudson

Place with fine views back down Loweswater. At the farm turn right in front of the house, ignoring the bridleway off to the left within a few yards, and instead walk downhill to the road junction by the Grange Hotel. Turn left along the lane and within a short distance take the turning right (fingerpost) up the access track to Graythwaite. Walk along the track as far as the first wall, then bear left beside this (fingerpost footpath to Sosgill).

The wall quickly becomes a fence, which is traced as far as a corner, and from there directly for a footbridge a few yards ahead. Cross this and go forward a few yards before turning sharp right along a faint footpath rejoining the farm track just below the house. Follow this left and round to gate, and beyond this passing to the rear of the house to cross a stile.

Turn immediately left up the edge of the field to a second stile. Cross this and, by bearing left again then right, follow a farm track with a fence on the right to negotiate yet another stile. Continue along the winding track uphill beneath a small pine wood, steepening towards the top of the hill. With the end of the walk now imminent, the walker may start to feel melancholy, perhaps, but the views from here back into the mountains evoke memories of the past two weeks' excellent trekking.

Over the rise the way levels along a fence line to a gate with Cockermouth town and Scotland beckoning in the far distance, the hills of Dumfries and Galloway rising as a nebulous backcloth to the Solway. Beyond the gate the way lies between hedges as far as a metalled lane. Turn left along this, passing High Mosser Farm. At the next farm pick up a footpath left signposted to Beech Hill. Immediately the farm is cleared, bear right through a gap in a hawthorn hedge, then head for the far bottom-left corner of the enclosure where a stile will be found.

Cross this and follow a fence downhill and around to the left, over a stile, and then climb towards a chapel. Pass this on its right side through two gates, then continue downhill with a fence on the left to reach and turn right along a metalled track. Follow this past the first junction on the right and the turning left soon afterwards, and later ignore the next right to continue forward in the direction of Blea Bank. Go round the bend in the road to pick up a footpath immediately on the right, following this slightly to the right to find a stile by a gate.

The central fells seen from the route to Mosser from Waterend

Go through this and straight forward, aiming for How Farm seen just over the crest of the rise, to pick up a step stile over a fence. Beyond this turn right and, within just a few paces, recross the fence and go straight forward, keeping the farm on the left to cross a further stile. Immediately beyond the stile turn left through a small gate and take a diagonal line to find a stile in the bottom corner of the small paddock, by a dew pond.

Here cross the footbridge and stile on the right and, keeping to the left edge of the pastures, cross a stile, follow the footpath into Hill Farm and from there proceed forward along the farm access track to the road. Turn left then immediately right and walk down the road for quarter of a mile to find a bridleway (signposted) for Low Hall taking off left at a gate just beyond a sweeping bend in the road.

A farm track from here is traced beside a hedge around the edge of a meadow, ignoring a gate on the right after 150 yards. When a second gate is met, turn right and walk forward a few yards, then go left (blue waymarking arrows), passing in front of the house and out along the access drive. Walk along this to the road at Green Trees, turn right then left after 200 yards, following the lane downhill for about half a mile to the site of the old Southwaite Mill.

Cross the bridge over the River Cocker and go through the stile on the left following a path alongside the river. At the second stile climb the banking and turn sharp left along the crest of this, overlooking the river and following the footpath onwards and downstream. >>

The Cocker was described by William in *The Prelude*, and whenever he recalled the river it transported him back to the days of his Cockermouth childhood. In a similar way, as we now follow the trail along its grassy banking, the Cocker takes us back to our beginnings at the end of the walk in the same town.

>> Soon a building comes into view. This is located on the site of the old Simonscales Mill. The route passes this on its right-hand side to reach a stile where a dirt track is intersected. Those wishing to camp in Cockermouth at the end of the walk should turn right up this track for half a mile and, after crossing the A66 town bypass, take the first turning on the right to reach the Violet Bank campsite and caravan park, which is on the left after a further 400 yards.

From the campsite the town centre is a 20-minute walk. Turn right out of the campsite, then right again into Simonscales Lane. After quarter of a mile turn left down Riverdale Drive and at the foot of the hill go left again into Dale View, following this around a right-hand bend to reach a footbridge over the River Cocker. Cross this and bear right up a stony track.

At the top of the hill continue ahead down the metalled road (Parkside Avenue) and at the junction bear right (A5086) then left (A595) almost immediately (signposted Wordsworth House), walking down Gallowbarrow into Sullart Street at the bottom. Wordsworth House is on the junction with Main Street at the foot of the hill.

Walkers continuing from Southwaite Mill along the riverside for the town centre or youth hostel should cross the track, leaving it by way of a second stile, the continuing path initially tracing a fence but soon bearing left to converge with the river. After a further quarter-mile the path passes beneath the A66, then shortly afterwards cuts diagonally across a wide loop of the Cocker to reach a footbridge. Turn left across this and left again for the youth hostel at Double Mill, otherwise follow the route from the bridge as described above to get to the town centre (a ten-minute walk).

USEFUL INFORMATION

Accommodation: Ample choice of hotel, guest-house and B&B accommodation in Cockermouth.

Camping: Violet Bank, Cockermouth. Open summer only. Full facilities. Fee £2.60/night/person.

Youth Hostel: Double Mills, Cockermouth, Cumbria, CA13 0DS. Tel: (01900) 822561.

Transport: Bus connections at Penrith for service X5 to Keswick and Cockermouth. Service No. 37 links Patterdale with Workington via Glenridding, Threlkeld, Keswick and Cockermouth.

Supplies: Good selection of stores in Cockermouth.

Refreshments: Several inns and cafés.

Tourist Information: Cockermouth: Market Street. Tel: (01900) 822634.

Useful Addresses and Contacts

Friends of National Parks, 246 Lavender Hill, London, SW11 1LJ. Tel: (0171) 924 4077.

Ramblers' Association, 1/5 Wandsworth Road, London, SW8 2XX. Tel: (0171) 582 6878.

The Backpackers' Club, PO Box 381, Reading, Berkshire, RG3 4RL. Tel: (01491) 680684.

Ordnance Survey, Romsey Road, Maybush, Southampton, Hants, SO9 4DH. Tel: (01703) 792000.

National Trust, The Hollens, Grasmere, Ambleside, Cumbria, LA22 9QZ. Tel: (015394) 35599

Long-Distance Walkers' Association, Secretary: Les Maple, 21 Upcroft, Windsor, Berkshire, SL4 3NH. Tel: (01753) 866685.

Countryside Commission, John Dower House, Crescent Place, Cheltenham, Glos, GL50 3RA. Tel: (01242) 521381.

Council for National Parks (CNP), 246 Lavender Hill, London, SW11 1LJ. Tel: (0171) 924 4077

Youth Hostels Association (YHA), Trevelyan House, 8 St Stephen's Hill, St Albans, Herts, AL1 2DY. Tel: (01727) 855215.

Lake District National Park Office, Brockhole, Windermere, Cumbria, LA23 1LJ. Tel: (015394) 46601

British Mountaineering Council (BMC), 177–79 Burton Road, Manchester, M20 2BB. Tel: (0161) 445 4747.

Friends of the Lake District, FREEPOST LA1186, Kendal, Cumbria, LA9 8BR.

Bowness Ferry Tel: (015394) 42753.

Cumbria Journey Planner Tel: (01228) 812812 or on the internet by accessing http://www.wwwebguides.com/pubtrans/cumbria/info.html

Lake District National Park 24-hour Weatherline Service Tel: (017687) 75757.

Lakeland Pick-and-Drop Service Tel: (016973) 44275/42768

National Trust free passenger shuttle. Enquiries Tel: (015394) 35599.

Railway travel information. Tel: (01539) 720397.

Ravenglass and Eskdale Steam Railway. Tel: (01229) 717171.

Stagecoach Cumberland. Tel: (01946) 63222.

Ullswater Lake Steamers. Tel: Glenridding (017684) 82229.

YHA summer-season shuttle bus. Enquiries Tel: (01727) 855215.

YOUTH HOSTELS

Ambleside: Waterhead, Ambleside, LA22 0EU, Cumbria. Tel: (015394) 32304. Bus routes 599, 555, 505, 506.

Black Sail: Black Sail Hut, Ennerdale, Cleator, Cumbria, CA23 3AY.

Borrowdale: Longthwaite, Borrowdale, Keswick, Cumbria, CA12 5XE. Tel:

(017687) 77257. Bus route 77A, 79.

Buttermere: King George VI Memorial Hostel, Buttermere, Cockermouth, Cumbria, CA13 9XA. Tel: (017687) 70245. Bus route 77, 77A.

Cockermouth: Double Mills, Cockermouth, Cumbria, CA13 0DS. Tel: (01900) 822561. Bus routes X5, 34, 35, 36.

Coniston: Coppermines House, Coppermines Valley, Coniston, Cumbria, LA21 8HP. Tel: (015394) 41261. Bus routes 505, 506.

Coniston: Holly How, Far End, Coniston, Cumbria, LA21 8DD. Tel: (015394) 41323. Bus routes 505, 506.

Elterwater (Langdale): Elterwater, Ambleside, Cumbria, LA22 9HZ. Tel: (015394) 37245.

Eskdale: Holmrook, Bleabeck, Cumbria, CA19 1TH. Tel: (019467) 23219.

Grasmere: Butterlip How, Grasmere, Ambleside, Cumbria, LA22 9QG. Tel: (015394) 35316. Bus routes 555, 599

Grasmere: Thorney How, Grasmere, Cumbria, LA22 9QW. Tel: (015394) 35591. Bus routes 555, 599.

Hawkshead: Esthwaite Lodge, Hawkshead, Ambleside, Cumbria, LA22 0QD. Tel: (015394) 36293. Bus routes 505, 506, 515.

Helvellyn: Greenside, Glenridding, Penrith, Cumbria, CA11 0QR. Tel: (017684) 8269. Bus route 108, 517.

Keswick: Station Road, Keswick, Cumbria, CA12 5LH. Tel: (017687) 72484. Bus route 555, X5.

Langdale: High Close, Loughrigg, Ambleside, Cumbria, LA22 9HJ. Tel: (015394) 37313.

Patterdale: Goldrill House, Patterdale, Penrith, Cumbria, CA11 0NW. Tel: (017684) 82394. Bus route 37, 517.

Windermere: High Cross, Bridge Lane, Troutbeck, Windermere, Cumbria, LA23 1LA. Tel: (015394) 43543. Bus routes 555, 505, 506 599.

CAMPSITES AND BUNKBARNS

Baysbrown campsite, Chapel Stile. Open in summer. £1.80/night/person. WC and sink but no shower. Also B&B at the farm.

Chapel Farm campsite, Longthwaite. Open all year. £2.50/night/person. Showers, WC and sinks. Enquiries to Gillercombe guest-house. Tel: (017687) 77602.

Coniston Hall (SD305961). Open in summer. £3/night/person. Shop, full wash facilities, showers, WC.

Cotgate campsite, Braithwaite. Open in summer. £2.70/night/person or £3.50 minimum. Full facilities plus shop and café. Tel: (017687) 78343.

Cragg Farm bunkbarn (NY173171), Buttermere. Open all year. £3/night/person.

Crook Farm campsite (SD284947), Torver. Open all year. £2/night/person. Shop, wash facilities, WC.

Dinah Hoggus camping barn, Rosthwaite. Open all year. £3/night/person. Tel: (017687) 77237.

Gillside Farm camping, Glenridding. Full facilities with farm produce available at house. Open March to mid-November. £4/night/person plus £1 for tent. Tel: (017684) 82346. A modern self-catering bunkhouse is also sited adjacent to Gillside Farm, open March to mid-November. Fee £6/night/person. Advance booking essential. Tel: (017684) 82346.

Great Langdale campsite, near the Old Dungeon Ghyll. Open all year. £3/night/person. Shop and full facilities.

Hillcroft Park campsite, Eamont Bridge. Open in summer. £4/night/person. Full facilities plus shop. Tel: (017684) 86363.

Hollins Farm campsite, Boot, Eskdale (NY178011). Open all year. £2/night/person. Showers, WC.

Lowther Park caravan and campsite, near Eamont Bridge. Open 17 March to 9 November inclusive. £3/night/person. Full facilities, including bar and supermarket. Tel: (017684) 863631.

Side Farm campsite, Patterdale. Open all year. £3.50/night/person. Full facilities, including small shop at farmhouse. Tel: (017684) 82337.

Sticklebarn bunkbarn, Great Langdale. Open all year. £10/night/person. Showers, toilets, drying room. Tel: (015394) 37356

Swirrel Bothy, Greenside, Glenridding. Tel: (017687) 72803.

Syke Farm campsite (NY173169), Buttermere. Open all year. £3/night/person. Showers, WC.

Sykeside campsite, Brotherswater Inn. Open all year. £1.80/night/person plus £1.80/tent. Full facilities, including shop, bar and restaurant. Tel: (017684) 82239.

Violet Bank caravan and campsite, Cockermouth (NY127294). Open summer. £2.60/night/person. Full wash facilities, WC and limited shop.

Wasdale Head campsite (NY187087). Open all year. £1.50/night/person. Nearby shop (open 0900–1730), WC.

Wasdale, National Trust campsite (NY183076). Open Easter to October. £3/night/person. Full wash facilities, WC, shop.

Waterside House campsite, near Eamont Bridge. Open summer. £4.50/night/person. Full facilities including shop.

OTHER ACCOMMODATION

The tourist information office in the relevant centre should be contacted for availability and phone numbers of hotels, guest-houses and B&B establishments. As with bunkbarns and hostels, walkers are advised to book ahead to guarantee a bed for the night.

TOURIST INFORMATION CENTRES

Ambleside: Church Street. Tel: (015394) 32582.
Ambleside: Waterhead Pier. Tel: (015394) 32729.
Bowness: Glebe Road. Tel: (015394) 42895.
Cockermouth: Market Street. Tel: (01900) 822634.
Coniston: Yewdale Road. Tel: (015394) 41533.
Grasmere: Red Bank Road. Tel: (015394) 35245.
Glenridding: Beckside Car Park. Tel: (017684) 82414.
Hawkshead: Main Car Park. Tel: (015394) 36525.
Keswick: Moot Hall. Tel: (017687) 72645.
Keswick: Discovery Centre. Tel: (017687) 72803.
Penrith: Middlegate. Tel: (017684) 72803.
Pooley Bridge: The Square. Tel: (017684) 86530.
Seatoller: Seatoller Barn (Borrowdale). Tel: (017687) 77294.
Windermere: Victoria Street. Tel: (015394) 46499.

Additional Attractions *en route*

Amazonia World of Reptiles, Windermere Quays Visitor Centre, Bowness. Tel: (015394) 48002. Collection of South American crocodiles, snakes, lizards and insects set in botanical garden where tropical birds freely nest. Turtle ponds. Open: All year except 25 December and 1 January, Monday to Saturday 9 a.m.–6 p.m., Sunday 11 a.m.–6 p.m.

Armitt Museum, Rydal Road, Ambleside. Tel: (015394) 33949. Interactive exhibition featuring Lakeland life, and history from the Bronze Age. Beatrix Potter's natural history watercolours, lantern slide show. Gift shop. Open: Daily from late summer, 10 a.m.–5 p.m.

Beatrix Potter Gallery, Main Street, Hawkshead. Tel: (01946) 63222. A National Trust exhibition featuring original drawings and illustrations from these popular children's stories. Open: 28 March to 2 November, Sunday to Thursday (closed Friday and Saturday, except Good Friday), 10.30 a.m.–4.30 p.m.

Cars of the Stars Motor Museum, Standish Street, Keswick. Interesting collection of original cars used in film and TV, including *Chitty Chitty Bang Bang*, the James Bond 007 cars, the Batmobile and Del Boy's Reliant Robin from the *Only Fools and Horses* series. Open: Spring half-term and then Easter to the end of December, 10 a.m.–5 p.m. every day.

Cumberland and Derwent Pencil Museum, Southey Works, Keswick. Tel: (017687) 73626. History of pencil-making, including discovery of local graphite deposits, cottage industry and modern pencil-making techniques. Open: All year every day (except 25, 26 December and 1 January), 9.30 a.m.–4 p.m.

Eskdale Corn-Mill, Boot, Holmrook. Tel: (019467) 23335. Evocative and well-preserved 16th-century corn-mill with two water-wheels. Also associated exhibits of milling machinery. Picnic area. Open: Easter to the end of September, Tuesday to Thursday 11 a.m.–5 p.m.

Hawkshead Grammar School, Hawkshead. Open: Easter to October. Monday to Saturday, 10 a.m.–12.30 p.m. and 1–5 p.m.; Sunday 1–5 p.m. October closing 4.30 p.m. Founded in 1585 and preserved just as it was when Wordsworth attended the school between 1779 and 1787.

Keswick Museum and Art Gallery, Station Road, Keswick, CA12 4NF. Tel: (017687) 73263. Exhibits featuring local geology, natural and local history. Open: Easter to October. Tuesday to Sunday and Bank Holiday Mondays 10 a.m.–4 p.m. (closed for lunch 12 noon–1 p.m.).

Penrith Town Museum, Robinson's School, Middlegate, Penrith. Tel: (01768) 864671. Listed building containing exhibits featuring geology, local history and archaeology of the Penrith area. Open: All year, June to September, Monday to Saturday, 10 a.m.–5 p.m., Sunday 1–5 p.m.; October to May, Monday to Saturday, 10 a.m.–5 p.m.

Ravenglass and Eskdale Steam Railway, Tel: (01229) 717171. Narrow-gauge railway linking the coast, at Ravenglass, with several stations in Eskdale, including Eskdale Green, Beckfoot and Dalegarth. Regular services (some steam) throughout the summer season with reduced service in winter. Café at Dalegarth terminus.

Rydal Mount, Rydal, Ambleside, Cumbria, LA22 9LU. Tel: (015394) 33002. Home of William Wordsworth from 1813 until his death in 1850. Contents include family portraits and personal possessions. The extensive gardens were landscaped by the poet. Gift shop. Open: March to October, every day: 9.30 a.m.–5 p.m., November to February, every day (except Tuesday): 10 a.m.–4 p.m.

Windermere Steamboat Museum, Rayrigg Road, Bowness. Tel: (015394) 45565. Houses a unique collection of historic steamboats and motor-boats, including SL *Dolly*, the oldest mechanically powered boat in the world. Kiosk open: Easter to October daily, 10 a.m.–5 p.m.

Wordsworth House, Main Street, Cockermouth. National Trust property. An elegant house with rooms furnished in keeping with the period, with some personal effects of the poet. Video display, shop with licence. Open: 26 March to 1 November weekdays only, 11 a.m.–5 p.m. Also on all Saturdays between 28 June and 6 September, and 25 October and 1 November. Closed remaining Saturdays and all Sundays. Last admission 4.30 p.m.

Wordsworth Museum and Dove Cottage, Town End, Grasmere, Ambleside. Tel: (015394) 35544/35547. Immaculately preserved home of William Wordsworth between 1799 and 1818 and adjoining museum with exhibits featuring original manuscripts, first editions and some personal belongings. Open: Daily between February and December 9.30 a.m.–5 p.m.; Closed: 6 January to 2 February (inclusive), 24 to 26 December. There is also an adjoining shop.